Incidents in a Life

Incidents in a Life

THE WAR IS OVER—I'D LIKE
A GLASS OF CHAMPAGNE

MARK PASCAL SCHLEFER

POSTERITY PRESS

ISBN 978-1-889274-54-6 (prime hardback)
ISBN 978-1-889274-55-3 (softcover)

Library of Congress Cataloging-in-Publication data:

Names: Schlefer, Mark Pascal, 1922- author.
Title: Incidents in a life : the war is over, I'd like a glass of champagne |
by Mark Pascal Schlefer.
Description: Chevy Chase, MD : Posterity Press, 2018.
Identifiers: LCCN 2018001369| ISBN 9781889274546 (alk. paper) |
ISBN 9781889274553 (alk. paper)
Subjects: LCSH: Schlefer, Mark Pascal, 1922- | Lawyers—Washington (D.C.)
—Biography. | Bombardiers—United States—Biography. | World War,
1939–1945—Personal narratives, American. | Freedom of information—
United States—History—20th century. | Maritime law—United States—
History—20th century.
Classification: LCC KF373.S339 A3 2018 |DCC 340.092 [B] —dc23

LC record available at https://lccn.loc.gov/2018001369

POSTERITY PRESS

PO Box 71002
Chevy Chase, MD 20813

Frontispiece photo by John Nopper

Printed in the United States of America

Contents

Prologue

THOSE OF MY GENERATION who saw combat in World War II (and were fortunate enough to survive) were changed by it, and I think the experience improved their characters. The immense responsibilities that were pressed upon them gave them a confidence and a stature that they might not have had if their young lives had been conventional. I say that from my own experience. As a very young twenty-two-year-old, my responsibilities became immense: to destroy targets on missions that our ground forces depended on for their very lives, and as lead bombardier-navigator to lead a formation of six bombers through antiaircraft flak that seemed to blacken the sky.

Consider one of the chapters that follows. I was ordered to navigate six airplanes across the South Atlantic in a nine-hour flight from Dakar, Senegal, in West Africa through the two-hundred-mile-thick dense cloud of the equatorial front, to Fortaleza, Brazil, utilizing pure dead-reckoning navigation with no radar and no checkpoints in the ocean. No airline today would give such a young person that kind of responsibility.

While combat experience matured us and strengthened who we were, it also taught us to live and work closely with men of very different backgrounds and education. I believe that doing all that changed and strengthened who I was and who I now am. In later life it never occurred to me that men and women in high positions in government or universities were not like me—that I should approach them on anything except an equal basis. You will read in one chapter that I, along with a friend, persuaded President Bill Clinton to sign the Comprehensive Nuclear-Test-Ban Treaty over the objection of the Pentagon. Another chapter relates how I defied a government agency that refused to explain its reasons for an important decision, a refusal that then led me to draft and help pass the landmark Freedom of Information Act, which President Lyndon Johnson signed only reluctantly.

The text that follows is a series of incidents—just that: incidents. Except for the introductory one, which is meant to set the stage, they are in approximate chronological order. My friends may think of this book as a memoir, but I never intended it to be that. For example, there is little in it about my wife, Marion, and our amazing life together for fully seventy years. What follows are isolated events, stories usually independent of each other. They are selected parts of my life— the life of a member of the World War II generation—which I thought might interest a reader. One can read them in any order. They lose no force by being read as one pleases: the war stories first, or the stories of my law practice—it matters not.

The incidents are based upon memory. Though I have tried to write as accurately as possible, memory is always fallible. Consider two examples:

First, for decades I remembered being on leave for a few days and staying in a hotel in Luxembourg. A bomb struck the hotel, knocked me out of bed, and made a wreck of the hotel. Unharmed, I picked my way through wreckage and got out unscathed. Some fifty years later, I was perusing letters I had written to Marion during the war; one was about this event. The letter described the hotel being in London, not Luxembourg.

Second, as I note in retelling the incident called "A Crash Landing and a Court-Martial," I remember that the Norden bombsight in my plane was destroyed. I cannot remember whether it was destroyed by the crash landing or whether I blew it up as we had standing orders to do—to prevent it from falling into enemy hands. It was a top-secret instrument, and we did not know whether we had landed on a German or an American airfield. It seems strange that the details of such a dramatic event should have been lost to my memory.

The following abbreviated details of my life and family may prove helpful to those who dip into these incidents in years to come:

I was born in 1922. During World War II, from 1943 to 1945, I was in the U.S. Army Air Force. A first lieutenant and bombardier-navigator, I was stationed in East Anglia,

England, and later in France, flying three dozen combat missions over German-held territory. I received my college degree with high honors in 1943 and my law degree in 1949, both from Harvard University. I practiced law, for a few years in New York City with the firm Paul, Weiss, Rifkind, Wharton & Garrison, and then for fifty-five years in Washington, D.C., with Radnor, Zito, Kominers & Fort, the firm that ultimately became Fort & Schlefer.

Marion King and I met on Bastille Day 1942, and we were married on April 9, 1944. Our first child, Jonathan, was born in 1949, Kate in 1951, and Ellen in 1955. Each child carries the name King as a middle name. Jonathan was educated at Harvard College and earned a PhD at MIT and an architectural degree at the University of California at Berkeley. Kate was educated at Yale College and received a law degree at Brooklyn Law School. Ellen was educated at the University of Chicago and the University of North Wales. She received a master's degree from Tuskegee College and a medical degree from Birmingham Medical School.

Marion's life and extraordinary accomplishments are told in summary form in her obituary, which I include as an epilogue. She graduated from Swarthmore College in 1945 with honors, greatly enjoyed the Harvard Graduate School of Design while I was at the Harvard Law School, and she later received an MA in art history from American University. Marion divided her time between the world of art and architecture and the economic aspects of housing and planning, as well as indulging in her passion for France and French. In Washington, she was on the board of the Metropolitan Washington Planning and Housing Association for twenty-five years and chair of the Committee of of 100 on the Federal City. She was on the Mayor's Committee on the Downtown, and worked for several architectural firms and for the Congressional Research Service as an analyst in housing and urban affairs.

Here I express my appreciation for the help, criticisms, and suggestions given me for this book by my wife and our children, Jonathan, Kate and Ellen, each in a different way, I also thank my friends Leonard Meeker and Arthur Westing. My title was suggested by my granddaughter, Molly Bicks.

King Farm
Putney, Vermont
October 2017

A Glass of Champagne

France, May 1945

THE WAR IN EUROPE was over on May 8, 1945, as I learned the next day, May 9, my twenty-third birthday. Our bomber group had not flown a combat mission in about ten days, we assumed because the front lines had moved beyond the range of B-26 Marauders carrying full bomb loads. On that day I found myself in Rheims because a general at SHAEF [Supreme Headquarters Allied Expeditionary Force] thought he might need an aide who knew German.

Having completed my check-in, I walked to the officers club, but was stopped at the door by a sergeant. "Sir, do you have a SHAEF card?"

"No, sergeant, I'm an officer in the 386th Bomb Group."

"I'm sorry, sir, this club is only for SHAEF officers." There was nothing to be gained by arguing with a sergeant.

"Sergeant, is there an officer in charge of this club?"

"Yes, sir."

"Would you please bring him to me."

"Yes, sir."

A few minutes later the sergeant returned with a captain.

It crossed my mind that here was an officer who had probably never been the target of enemy fire. I had flown eleven missions more than the normal tour of twenty-five because of the high mortality rate among bombardier-navigators who sat in the Plexiglass nose of the Marauders. Yet I was only a first lieutenant.

"Captain, my name is Mark Schlefer. I'm a bombardier-navigator attached to the 386th Bomb Group. I've flown thirty-six combat missions over enemy territory. The war here was over yesterday. Today is my twenty-third birthday and I'd like a glass of champagne to celebrate both events."

The captain put his arm around my shoulder and said warmly, "Be my guest, Lieutenant."

Unknown to me at the time, an atomic bomb was shortly to be exploded in a test in a New Mexico desert. The possibility of nuclear war cast a shadow in the minds of the more thoughtful members of my generation.

PART ONE

AND THE WAR CAME

Founding family: Great Uncle Henry stands at right, beside my grandmother Pepi in 1888.

How I Accidently Got Myself into the Ethical Culture Fieldston School

New York City, 1928

WHEN I WAS SIX YEARS OLD my family moved to 320 West End Avenue at 75th Street in New York City, and I was entered in the nearby public school. The teacher started each day with the Pledge of Allegiance. When I was seven years old I refused to join the others in the Pledge. What possessed this seven-year-old boy to refuse so simple a ritual I have no idea. He was punished by being forced to stand facing the corner. He persisted. Finally the teacher, exasperated, asked my mother to come in to talk to her about her son's conduct. I infer or was told that Mother thought the lady was an idiot.

She told my father she wanted to put me into the Ethical Culture Fieldston School, which had a branch nearby. Dad demurred, saying he had gone to Boys' High in Brooklyn, learned to read Virgil's *Aeneid* in Latin and do calculus— and what was good enough for him was good enough for his son. Mother, who must have already wanted to move me, suggested he talk to the teacher. When he returned he agreed, "All right, send him to the Ethical Culture School," which I then attended from the third grade through the twelfth. It was an extraordinary educational experience.

My Debut at the Met

New York City, 1938

I WAS A POOR SINGER, a monotone singing by myself. When I was in high school I nevertheless appeared on stage in an elegant evening performance of *Aida* in the old Metropolitan Opera House on West 39th Street. This is how it happened.

School let out early on Wednesdays and from time to time I saved up 55 cents and went see a matinee at the WPA (Works Progress Administration) Theater. Somehow I learned that at the Met you could volunteer to be a "super" (i.e., supernumerary) by standing outside the stage door where someone would come out and select several people as needed for the opera. I tried this for several cold evenings until I was finally selected. The stipend was $2, serious money when my daily allowance was 25 cents and subway fare was a nickel.

The backstage of the opera house was filthy beyond belief, so unlike the glittering "Diamond Horseshoe." The Egyptian soldier's clothes that I was asked to don were as dirty as everything else in that strange locker room. Most surprising, I saw men "in drag" for the first time—in the locker room, men dressing as women, using lipstick and wearing earrings and necklaces.

My job was to hold one of four corners of a platform that bore a statue of a bull and carry it across the stage. While I was tall, the other three men were stronger. At one point I thought I might drop my corner in the middle of the stage.

But I held on, and I was able to hear the entire opera. When I got home I took a long deep bath.

Dr. Pascal and the Pascal Family

New York City circa 1940
Romania until 1888

WHEN I WAS ABOUT EIGHTEEN years old I went for a check-up to Dr. Pascal—Uncle Henry, my great uncle and our family physician. His office was in a brownstone off Central Park West. When you entered, a Catholic nun escorted you to what would have been the living room in a private house, and she settled you down with a *National Geographic* to read.

When the doctor was ready to see you, she led you through the sliding chestnut doors to what would have been the dining room. At the far end was a little stage with the doctor's desk on it and Uncle Henry sitting at his desk, a stained glass window behind him. The building was on the south side of the street and hence the sun shown through the stained glass window. Uncle Henry looked more like God than Charles Evans Hughes.

There was no familiar greeting. He took your temperature and blood pressure and looked at your throat. If he wanted to examine you without clothes, you went to the next room, which would have been the kitchen in a private house.

Then back to his desk. There he made some notes with a pen that had three different colors of ink, used presumably for different purposes.

Then for the first time a warm greeting: "Well Mark, how are your brother and your mother and father? You know Mark you should try to give up smoking. We do not know why, but smoking is bad for your lungs and your heart. (This was long before the Surgeon General's report on smoking.)

"More important, don't let any habit tell you what to do. You should never let yourself become subject to a habit—even eating. You should be able to give up a meal once in a while."

Uncle Henry once gave me a book by Walter Lippmann that he thought I should read. He did not believe in an afterlife or in any formal religion. He left Judaism and joined the Ethical Culture Society. That may have been the reason my mother wanted to send me to the Ethical Culture Fieldston School. Uncle Henry deliberately over-charged his wealthy patients so that he could serve those with less income.

Harlem Hospital had had only white physicians. In the 1920s Uncle Henry put black physicians on the staff. In time, the board of the hospital became half white and half black. Mayor Jimmy Walker and Tammany Hall opposed the integration of blacks. This was fifty years before the civil rights movement. Uncle Henry resigned and joined St. Elizabeth Hospital as its chief surgeon, bringing black physicians with him. Catholics were more tolerant of blacks.

According to my cousin Joan Pascal Karasik's history—
The Pascals: An Immigrant History—my great grandfather,
Pesach Pascal emigrated from Romania to America on
August 28, 1888. He brought seven of his children, including
Uncle Henry and Henry's younger brother Uncle Joe, as
well as my Grandmother Pepi, and siblings Sara, Rose, and
Isadore. Pascal is a Spanish name, and they might have been
Sephardic Jews who moved to Romania when their ancestors
were expelled from Spain in 1492 (though Cousin Joan
wrote that a few Jews lived in what is now Romania as far
back as the Roman Empire).

In Romania, my great grandfather, Pesach Pascal, had
owned and operated a large farm. Uncle Henry said that
they had forty or fifty laborers. My mother told me it was a
4,000-acre farm, which she thought he rented from a
member of the aristocracy. The Pascals spoke Romanian and
Yiddish as well as some French and German. They were
well-educated people, and quite prosperous. At one point
they had to move to the small city of Piatra, where Pesach
became one of the prominent citizens and an agent for the
state lottery.

In the 1880s anti-Semitism spread in Europe. Jews were
excluded from schools and universities and from certain
occupations. All this prompted the Pascals to emigrate:
eight to the United States, one to Canada, and one to Paris
(the latter two of whom I met). There were still others:

Pesach Pascal had thirteen children, and I think I heard from my mother that some went to Brazil.

Cousin Joan describes how Uncle Henry learned to speak English, worked his way through medical school, graduated first in his class winning a check for $100. He interned at Bellevue Hospital and became a surgeon. Uncle Henry's younger brother Joe graduated from City College of New York, went to New York Law School, and became corporation counsel of New York City. He served for forty years; he drafted the contracts for the Third Avenue El and the George Washington Bridge, as well as many others. Other Pascal immigrants all prospered in the New World—except for Uncle Isadore who was a crook and served time.

My great grandfather's portrait presides proudly in my living room today.

The Depression, the Coming War and Archibald MacLeish

New York City, Route 66 and Cambridge, 1930–1941

IT IS ALMOST IMPOSSIBLE to convey the economic suffering that pervaded the nation in the 1930s. I was eight years old in 1930 and remember the visible signs of the Depression. We lived one block from Riverside Drive on the Upper West Side of Manhattan. Just beyond Riverside Drive was fill dirt extending into the Hudson River, and in the center of the fill dirt was a deep trench. At the bottom of the trench ran railroad tracks that carried freight trains destined for Albany, Buffalo, Cleveland, and Chicago. The West Side Drive was still in the future.

Beyond the tracks on the fill dirt was a "Hooverville," a shantytown named for President Hoover and thrown up by veterans of "the Great War," as World War I was called. They lived in shacks of discarded highway billboards, scrap lumber, and other reusable trash. What they used for plumbing, fresh water, and other necessities of life I have no idea—perhaps the Hudson River. They had a flagpole and they raised the flag in the morning and brought it down at sunset to the bugled tune of "Taps." (This was long before the modern custom of leaving a flag up all night with a spotlight shining to evoke "The Star-Spangled Banner." Bob McNamara once told me he instituted the new practice at Robert Kennedy's request; Bob didn't think it was a great idea, but he put it through because as defense secretary he had more important issues to debate with the attorney general.)

There were other visible signs of the Depression. At Central Park West a few stands announced, "Mrs. William Randolph Hearst's Milk Fund." So-called apple men sold apples for a nickel all over the city. Shoeshine boys polished shoes for a dime. One day I saw John D. Rockefeller as he drove down Broadway in an open limousine on his ninety-second birthday, throwing dimes out to the scrambling public. (I couldn't join the fray because I was forbidden to walk or play in the street!) He had been pronounced dead on his birthday by his life insurance company which then paid him the face value of his policies.

There was no unemployment insurance, no Medicaid, no Medicare, no welfare—only private charity. Except for the Chinese Exclusion Act of 1882, there had been no limit on immigration until 1920, only ten years before the onset of the Depression. New York was a city of millions of immigrants, who generally thought that the Bank of United States was the U.S. government bank and thus absolutely safe. It was not, and there was no federal bank deposit insurance. Millions of immigrants (and others) lost all their savings when the bank failed.

I was two months shy of my eleventh birthday when Franklin Delano Roosevelt was inaugurated as president on March 4, 1933. The unemployment rate was 30 percent and had been for several years—a huge number (compared with 10 percent at the height of the recession after the 2007–2009 financial crisis). When President Roosevelt said he saw "one-third of our nation ill-housed, ill-clothed, and ill-fed," he was talking of the unemployed.

Six years later, in the summer of 1939, I and two friends, Warren Paley and Richard Sprayregen, drove across the country following Route 66 as charted in *The Grapes of Wrath*, John Steinbeck's powerful novel of wanderers to the West Coast from the Dust Bowl of the Midwest. We slept in farmers' fields and cooked out, then we returned via a northern route.

On September 1, Adolf Hitler, having previously seized Czechoslovakia's Sudetenland, invaded Poland and occupied Danzig in defiance of British prime minister Neville Chamberlain's latest ultimatum. Staying at the YMCA in Chicago, after reading the famous peace passage from Isaiah in a Gideons Bible, I wrote a letter to my parents: "They shall beat their swords into plowshares, and their spears into pruning hooks; nation shall not lift up sword against nation, neither shall they learn war any more." I predicted there would be no war; there could be no war. But the war did come. Two days later, on September 3, Britain and France declared war on Germany.

Ten days later I started my freshman year at college. The Harvard class of 1943 came from across the United States and elsewhere. My roommate in Matthews Hall came from Racine, Wisconsin. Across the corridor, George Kelton came from Radnor, Pennsylvania, and his roommate, George Fowler, lived in Everett, Washington. These were typical of the 977 members of the class who convened in the Freshman Union in Harvard Yard to be welcomed by university president James Conant, deans William L. Sperry and Richard Gummere, and Mr. Archibald MacLeish.

The *Freshman Red Book* for the class mentions the substance of the talks by the first three, but was silent about MacLeish. He had been trained as a lawyer at the Harvard Law School and practiced for a time, but soon became a writer and poet, spending half a dozen years in Paris in the 1920s. There he may have acquired his intense antipathy for fascism. On his return to the United States, as a writer and editor he became interested in politics. In 1939, President Roosevelt appointed him the Librarian of Congress.

MacLeish opened his talk by comparing the class of 1943 to the class of 1917. He opined that our class would not graduate from college as a group. The war would cause the breakup of the class, he said. Some would never return, while others would later return to complete their studies after the war was over.

The talk was greeted with dead silence. Not a single clap in applause was heard. Young men, almost one thousand strong from many backgrounds and places—young men who had graduated from Groton and Exeter and high schools in Missoula, Montana, and elsewhere—all reacted as a single unit. We had been brought up on Benjamin Franklin's 1783 aphorism "There was never a good war or a bad peace," and on widespread feelings of near-pacifism and isolationism following the horrors of World War I. But the class was as wrong as I had been in my letter from the YMCA weeks earlier. And MacLeish was right. The class did not graduate as a unit, and thirty-three members gave their lives in the war that MacLeish had talked about.

Pearl Harbor Day

Cambridge, December 7, 1941

ON THE FIRST SUNDAY in December, I was in my room in Kirkland House playing bridge with three friends and listening to the New York Philharmonic. My partner was Lloyd Shapley, who in 2012 would win the Nobel Prize in Economic Sciences. Suddenly, the symphony stopped and the orchestra played "The Star-Spangled Banner." An announcer came on and declared that the Empire of Japan had bombed Pearl Harbor. None of us knew where Pearl Harbor was. The next day President Roosevelt came on national radio and made his famous address, his "Date of Infamy" speech, asking Congress to declare war on the Japanese Empire.

As soon as we had a chance to think about it, almost everyone at Harvard College, and indeed in much of the United States, worried that the force and might of the United States would be concentrated in the Far East. The summer before, I had worked in New York as a volunteer for the Fight for Freedom Committee, an organization that supported aid to Britain and opposed the much stronger America First Committee. We thought that Western civilization was at stake in Europe, where Britain was standing heroically alone against Nazi Germany and Fascist Italy. America was still isolationist in foreign affairs; we would never have entered the war unless attacked.

We were in suspense all day Monday and Tuesday. President Conant spoke on closed-circuit radio to the university on Tuesday evening, emphasizing that Europe was still the major concern. We knew that Hitler had a mutual defense treaty with Japan, but he had breached his treaty with the Soviet Union. He might thus do the same with Japan. Then Wednesday afternoon the news came that Hitler had declared war on the United States. The suspense during those three days, Sunday to Wednesday, was memorable, but I have not seen it reported in any history of World War II.

Marion—How We Met

Cambridge, Bastille Day 1942

ALMOST EVERY DAY THROUGH high school I rode the subway to school and back with a friend, Jeff DeWald, who later went on to Haverford College. When summer approached in 1942 he wrote me a note suggesting that I look up Marion King as she and I would both be attending Harvard Summer School: "She is stunningly beautiful and brilliant." I called her and we agreed to meet on Bastille Day in front of Straus Hall at the corner of Harvard Yard. I arrived first and saw her walking toward me along the path in front of Wigglesworth Hall: her beauty, grace and intelligence were radiant. I fell in love before we exchanged a word.

It was not at first mutual. Swains flocked around her like moths around a flame. I wooed her by reading poetry—Emily Dickinson, T. S. Eliot, Shakespeare, and John Donne: "I wonder by my troth, what thou, and I / did till we lov'd? were we not wean'd till then? / But suck'd on country pleasures, childishly?"

We walked the streets of Cambridge and in Mount Auburn Cemetery we read the gravestones of famous people buried there. I think—although Marion never told me this—that she thought, "If he reads poetry to me, walks the streets with me, explores the cemetery with me, then that is the kind of person I want to spend the rest of my life with."

We always treated Bastille Day as our real anniversary.

Alfred North Whitehead, Eleanor Roosevelt and I.F. Stone

Cambridge and Washington, 1942–1988

THE WORLD IN 1942 presented a grim outlook. Japan, under a repressive tyranny, had invaded Manchuria, held the Korean peninsula under its military heel, and had attacked the United States, destroying much of our fleet at Pearl Harbor. Joseph Stalin held Russia and several other countries in his grip; the Soviet Union was termed a prison of nations. Hitler and National Socialism dominated most of Europe from Norway, the Low Countries, and France to Yugoslavia and Greece. In Italy, Benito Mussolini's Fascist state joined Hitler's military Axis. Francisco Franco and his breed of fascism ruled Spain. Portugal also was under the grip of a tyrant.

I was politically active from the time I arrived at college in 1939, joining the Harvard Student Union. On November 30, 1939, the Soviet Union invaded Finland. A debate arose within the Student Union whether to condemn the invasion. Communist sympathizers opposed the motion to condemn. At a stormy meeting in the Lowell House common room that lasted until two in the morning, those opposed won by one vote, counting the vote of a member who was confined to Stillman Infirmary and not present at the meeting. Along with others, I broke from the Student Union and formed the Harvard Liberal Union. In subsequent years I became an editor of the Harvard Guardian, a political magazine; vice president of the Liberal Union; and even a labor organizer at Bethlehem Steel's Fore River Shipyard.

The Liberal Union sponsored many talks and discussion programs, including several that featured Eleanor Roosevelt. She invited the organization's officers—Roger Fisher, Louis Pollak, Adam Yarmolinsky, and me—to come to Washington to meet her husband, the president. We rode the train to Washington (the fare was five dollars) where we four kids astonished a taxi driver by directing him to take us to the White House, and the guards admitted us without any form of identification. Mrs. Roosevelt greeted us downstairs and took us up to the family quarters, where the president received us wearing a bow tie and enjoying a martini. Ever since, I have worn bow ties and enjoyed a martini at cocktail time.

(I should mention that we all went to bigger things. Roger worked on the Marshall Plan under Averill Harriman, practiced law at Covington & Burling, and became a professor at Harvard Law School. Louis served as dean of both Yale Law School and the University of Pennsylvania Law School before becoming a federal judge. Adam, my friend from elementary school onward, held high positions in the Kennedy, Johnson, and Carter administrations.)

My political activities aside, at Harvard I was enrolled in the American History and Literature program, which required readings outside of the main curriculum. These included eight books each of the Old Testament and New Testament, Homer's epics, several classical Greek plays and histories, and some readings in Plato and Aristotle. We had to take oral examinations administered by professors in the departments of classics, philosophy, or other relevant areas. Professor Alfred North Whitehead examined me on Plato's *Republic*.

I was not at the time aware of Whitehead's fame and importance to philosophy. I had never heard of his and Bertrand Russell's *Principia Mathematica*, their attempt to found all logical statements on a set of coherent axioms. During the oral examination I attacked the society that Plato envisioned as a fascist oligarchy that bred humans like cattle to improve their offspring and took children from their parents to train them with falsehoods about an unreal world of supposed perfection. That world was run by philosopher kings, selected by a method Plato never disclosed, but certainly not by popular vote.

Plato hated Athens and glorified Sparta. Sparks flew during the hour-long examination, and when I left I said to myself, "Well, I blew that one."

Whitehead must have thought, "At least the young fellow read the *Republic*, thought about it, and some day may appreciate its significance." I passed the exam with high honors.

Two books, separated by some fifty-five years of life, made me reflect much later on that oral examination. One was a book I read in East Anglia between flying bombing missions over German-controlled territory. In a library for servicemen, I found Whitehead's 1933 *Adventures of Ideas*. It was a beautifully written book, full of new ideas for me. In it I discovered a line that explained the controversy in my oral examination: "All of philosophy is but a footnote to Plato." Philosophy that sprang from mathematics was likely to embrace the internal perfection of the *Republic*. Democracy, as a friend once observed, is "messy," disorganized and confusing, while striving for symmetry and order leads to dictatorship.

Fifty-five years later I read *The Trial of Socrates* by the muckraking journalist I. F. Stone, who wrote that he could not understand why the first great democracy put its greatest philosopher to death. Stone taught himself ancient Greek in order to read all the surviving original sources relating to Socrates's trial, conviction, and execution.

Most of what Stone found about Socrates came from Plato's *Dialogues*. Stone found that Socrates had taught his students—Plato among them—to seek the ideal in Sparta and detest the democracy of Athens. A number of his students deserted Athens for Sparta during the Peloponnesian War. "Absolutism is the hallmark of the Platonic utopias," Stone wrote. He found that in the Laws Plato envisioned an "inquisitorial body empowered to root out dissent, the archetype of our late, but unlamented House Un-American Activities Committee" and entrenched it in his utopia. The Laws of Plato "were in fact the first sketches of what we now call totalitarian societies," Stone wrote. At last a serious scholar had borne out my sophomoric attack on the *Republic* in my oral examination with Professor Whitehead.

What Day for the Wedding?

New York City, 1944

A SHAVETAIL WITH NEW GOLD bars but no unit assignment, I was given about two weeks leave and Marion and I decided to get married, almost two years after we first met on Bastille Day in 1942.

Neither my family nor Marion's family was religious. In fact Marion's father, Howard Langdon King, would not let her go to Sunday School as her childhood friends did. He would rather spend Sundays on one of the Long Island beaches identifying shore birds. My family also paid little attention to religion. When I was sixteen and applied to Harvard College, one of the questions on the application was, "What is your religion?" (I hope they don't ask that now!) My response, in bold letters, was "NONE." We never paid much attention to religious holidays.

My leave was short and it appeared that Friday would be the earliest day for the wedding, but Howard opposed it. "You cannot have the wedding on Good Friday. That is when Jesus was crucified." So we proposed to wait until

Saturday. But my father, John Jacob "Jack" Schlefer, opposed that because it was the Sabbath, although he never before paid attention to Saturday as the Sabbath. So we all compromised on April 9, Easter Sunday!

What it all meant was that Howard thought of himself culturally as a Christian and my father thought of himself culturally as a Jew. We were married at the Ethical Culture School at 64th Street and Central Park West, standing by ourselves with no maid of honor and no best man.

We took a train to Boston and then a boat to Nantucket. We both loved *Moby Dick*. The Whaling Museum was closed until June. I got in touch with the curator and asked him to open it for us, which he did. (In 1994 we returned to Nantucket for our fiftieth anniversary with our children.)

It bears mention that neither Marion nor I believed in God or in an afterlife. But she thought of herself as a Christian and I have always been proud of my Hebraic background.

The wedding took place in the middle of a great war and there was no champagne—but despite that our marriage lasted seventy years.

PART TWO

A Bombardier in World War II

Lt. Christiansen (pilot), Lt. Haas (co-pilot), Lt. Schlefer (bombardier-navigator), Cpl. Funk, Cpl. O'Kelly, Cpl. Hamlet (gunners)

9

The Knife

Texas, 1944

I HAD JUST GRADUATED from cadet training school in Midland, Texas, and was wearing my new gold bars for the first time, with orders to report to gunnery training school in Laredo, Texas. Taking a public bus to Laredo, I was sitting in an aisle seat. Across the aisle was an empty seat beside a GI in the window seat who sat cleaning his fingernails with a jackknife. A black soldier boarded the bus and was about to occupy the empty seat across the aisle from me.

"Nigger," said the GI, "if you sit in that seat you'll never get up."

"Soldier," I said, almost without thinking, "give me that knife, right now." The soldier complied without a word.

And then to the black soldier, I said, "Sit in my seat, soldier."

I moved across the aisle and took the seat next to the soldier whose knife I had taken. I said, "You can recover your knife from the commanding officer of the Laredo gunnery school, after you tell him why I took it from you."

I must say that I was not a little frightened at my own sudden action, my first order as an officer given almost without thinking.

After arriving at the gunnery school I delivered the knife to the CO with an explanation of what had happened. I never did find out whether the GI recovered it. Nor do I remember how anyone else on the bus—white people in the Deep South where strict segregation reigned—reacted to this incident involving three soldiers wearing their country's uniform.

10

Greenland's Icecap and the Perfect Lawn

En Route to the European Theater of Operations, July 1944

A FEW WEEKS AFTER the Normandy landings, the crew of our B-26 Marauder picked up our plane at Tampa, Florida, and, after a few checkout flights, received orders to proceed to Northern Ireland in easy stages by way of Maine, Canada, Greenland, Iceland, and Scotland.

At 54 degrees north latitude, Goose Bay, Labrador, is a good deal closer to the North Pole than to the Equator. We arrived only a few weeks past midsummer, when there were only a few hours of darkness on either side of midnight.

Our next stop was the Bluie West airfield on the west coast of Greenland, two hundred or so miles north of Cape Farewell at the southern tip of Greenland. The airfield lay at the end of a long fjord, the sides of which rose above a cloud bank that hovered perpetually at about six thousand feet. The pilot had to fly between the walls of the fjord and below the cloud cover.

There were a number of dead ends to the left and right that could be mistaken for the main course of the fjord. If the plane were flown into one of the dead ends, the plane and all aboard would be lost. There would not be space or time to make a U-turn or increase altitude to clear the fjord walls. The pilot, Herb Christiansen, copilot Don Haas and I, as bombardier-navigator, spent hours and hours viewing and re-viewing a film of the fjord, memorizing its geography that led forty or fifty miles from the open sea to Bluie West. At the end of the fjord, just beyond the airfield, rose the Greenland icecap—ice some two miles thick, which at its highest reached twelve thousand feet above sea level. The airfield was on a slope: downhill, west toward the water; uphill, east toward the icecap. Planes landed uphill and took off downhill regardless of the direction of the wind.

After one or two nights at Goose Bay, we took off for Bluie West. Shortly after taking off, Haas called me where I was sitting at the navigation desk behind the pilots. "I see a mountain on the horizon," he said over the intercom.

"You must be dreaming," I replied. "The Greenland icecap is at least four hundred miles away. At six thousand feet you cannot possibly see a mountain four hundred miles away."

A few minutes later Haas called again, "Come up here and see for yourself." He was right: a mountain was clearly visible.

Recalculating my course and distances, I remained puzzled. Perhaps the clarity of the air and the lack of dust to collect moisture might be the reason. The trouble with this explanation was that I thought—although I could not calculate it—that at six thousand feet the curvature of the earth would preclude seeing a mountain four hundred miles away.

As it turned out, we flew for well over two hours at 180 miles per hour until we got to the fjord.

About sixty-five years later, reading Tim Severin's *The Brendan Voyage*, Marion came across the probable explanation for the strange vision we had had of the mountain four hundred miles away. It must have been the so-called Arctic mirage.

Severin wrote: "The Arctic mirage, known in Iceland as the hillingar effect, is the northern equivalent of the well-known desert mirage. The Arctic mirage occurs when a stable mass of clear air rests on a much colder surface. The result is to change the optical properties of the air so that it bends the light like a giant lens. Objects far beyond the normal horizon appear within view floating above the horizon, and sometimes appear upside down and stacked one image above the other. Sextant readings become unreliable and the theoretical horizon may extend for a distance limited only by the resolution of the human eye. Highly favorable conditions for the Arctic mirage occur over Greenland, where a mass of high-pressure heavy air rests on the great icecap, while the high-altitude Greenland glaciers supply the bright source of reflected light for the mirage."

Having navigated the fjord, we spent one night at Bluie West and took off over the icecap for Iceland. We had been warned that while the icecap appeared from the air to be an endlessly smooth white surface, it was in fact peppered with huge boulders of ice. We were also warned that a German submarine off Cape Farewell, Greenland, was broadcasting a radio signal to attract ships. But we landed at Reykjavik in Iceland without mishap. Again we spent a night before taking off for Scotland, then flying westward to Northern Ireland for more training in pilotage navigation over foreign terrain, navigating by relying on visible landmarks. (In Texas, for example, railroads were rare and reliably ran east-west for easy orientation; in Europe railroads were common and ran in all directions. Rather than depend on train tracks, in Northern Ireland we learned to study the shapes of forest edges, which across Europe remained unchanged for generations. We practiced honoring boundaries too, and not crossing into the airspace of the neutral Irish Republic.)

A high point of this amazing journey was a couple of days in Prestwick, Scotland, where we stayed in a medieval castle, with crenellated battlements and towers. An extraordinarily beautiful lawn surrounded the castle. Walking around the castle, I came upon an elderly man working on the lawn. I asked him, "What does it take to create such a lovely grass lawn?"

"Well, sir," he replied, "if you seed the lawn every day, fertilize it every day, roll it every day, and cut it every day, in a hundred years you'll have a lawn like this."

Britain, in a desperate war for survival, still found it worthwhile to seed, fertilize, roll, and cut this piece of land—this grass—every day!

11

A Bridge Too Far, A Message Too Quick

East Anglia, England, and Arnhem, Holland, September 1944

WE WERE ASSIGNED to the 386th Bomb Group, based in Great Dunmow Station, East Anglia. By September, the Allies were on the march. Paris had been liberated, and General George Patton was already racing across France toward the Siegfried Line and the Rhine River. Field Marshal Bernard Montgomery conceived a plan to invade Holland over the Rhine highway bridges. If successful, the army would not only liberate Holland before the winter, but also move up the far side of the Rhine and outflank the Germans. It was the stroke needed to destroy the German army and win the war in 1944.

Generals George Patton, Omar Bradley, and Dwight Eisenhower all opposed Montgomery's idea as being too risky. In Holland the Rhine divides into two branches. The northern branch flows toward Arnhem and is called the Lower Rhine. The southern branch flows toward Nijmegen and is called the Waal River. Each then flows separately to the North Sea. There were two bridges for the Allies to cross: the Arnhem Bridge over the northern branch and the

Nijmegen over the southern branch, offering a double opportunity for German tanks to counterattack the narrow British army column as it went over each bridge. In his excellent 1974 book, *A Bridge Too Far*, Cornelius Ryan reveals that under pressure from British Prime Minister Winston Churchill, Eisenhower agreed to permit Montgomery to carry out his plan.

The attack on Holland turned into a major disaster. German Panzer divisions crushed the attack, and Montgomery's troops recrossed the highway bridges. The mission of the 386th Bomb Group was to destroy Arnhem Bridge after the British retreated. Our early and complete briefing made clear that the bridge must be destroyed to prevent the German troops and tanks from following.

Although it was only my fourth mission, our plane was in the lead position, possibly because bombardier-navigators were in short supply and many planes lacked them. (In those Marauders without bombardier-navigators, the bombs were released by "togglers," enlisted men who watched the lead plane and flipped toggle switches to release their loads when they saw the lead plane's bombs fall.)

To appreciate the extraordinary event that occurred on this mission, it is necessary to understand the structure of the radio system on all B-26 Marauders in Europe. Each Marauder had radios set with four channels: "A" channel was for communications within its group; "B" channel reached

Bomber Command; "C" channel called Fighter Command; and "D" channel was a kind of emergency channel. The frequencies of the channels were changed daily on the radios in each plane in the middle of the night by an enlisted man who knew only how far to move the dial; he did not know the actual frequencies, which were highly guarded secrets at Ninth Air Force headquarters. The group frequency, "A" channel, was different for each of the hundreds of groups in the European theater of operations.

As we approached the so-called "initial point," and before the squadrons assembled in three multidirectional approaches to the target, a clear Women's Army Corps (WAC) voice— or at least what sounded like one—came over "A" channel: "This is Bomber Command. This is Bomber Command. The mission has been called off. Return to your base."

Had our troops recovered their positions? Did the Allies now need the bridge? Someone called out on "A" channel, "Can you tell us the colors of the day?" The presumed WAC failed to answer. Another radio operator checked with Bomber Command on "B" channel.

"No. Proceed with your mission," he was told. That we did, and blew up the bridge.

Clearly the first message had been bogus. How had the Germans known the group frequency? The "A" channel frequency had, as usual, been changed in the middle of the night.

A similar event happened another time. Our colonel was a valuable asset. Bomber Command would not let him fly missions except on rare occasions. On one mission when the colonel was flying, German antiaircraft shot down three of the group's planes. They called up on "A" channel, "How's that for shooting, Colonel Corbin?" The Germans not only knew the group frequency, but they knew that the colonel was flying on the mission!

It was the kind of security breach that made us lose sleep.

12

A Crash Landing and a Court-Martial

France, November 1944

AFTER OUR UNIT was relocated to an airfield at Beaumont-sur-Oise, north of Paris, our plane's pilot, copilot, and I were court-martialed for destruction of government property—our bomber and its bombsight.

In November of 1944, the skies over northern Europe were generally covered with cold, gray clouds. Thousands of warplanes—at least the medium bombardment groups of the Ninth Air Force—were grounded through most of the autumn. Our 386th Bomb Group did not fly a single mission from October 14 to November 10. Meanwhile, a million Allied soldiers, marshaled in five armies under generals Jacob Devers, Courtney Hodges, George Patton, and Omar Bradley, as well as Field Marshal Bernard Montgomery, were locked in combat on the western front of the Third Reich. After the landings at Normandy in June, the armies had raced across France and parts of Belgium until halted by the Siegfried Line or they outran supplies or fuel. Now they were deprived of bomber support by the weather.

Normally, missions were called for early morning. The briefing would begin at about six o'clock and takeoff would start at seven thirty or eight, permitting ample daylight to complete the mission. But in November, darkness comes early in northern Europe, which is roughly on the same latitude as Newfoundland, Canada, more than a thousand miles north of the continental United States. The winter night falls early and quickly.

It is understandable in view of the persistent bad weather that on rare clear days the Ninth Air Force Bomber Command ordered late-afternoon missions against tactical targets in support of the five stalled Allied armies. But one cause of my "destruction" of U.S. government property that precipitated the court-martial was the lateness of a bombing mission one November day.

Twin-engine planes like our group's B-26 Marauders successfully attacked small targets such as bridges, ammunition dumps, railroad marshaling yards, supply depots, petroleum tank farms, communication centers, and gun positions. These missions, such as the permanent destruction of bridges over the Rhine, demanded great precision. Merely bombing and destroying the roadway suspended between the piers of a bridge permitted the German army to replace the artery in a matter of weeks. We were therefore ordered to destroy the piers themselves.

A bridge pier is a tiny target from the twelve- to thirteen-thousand-foot altitude at which we flew. But it was the optimum altitude for the accuracy of the Norden bombsight, a remarkable instrument that enabled our high degree of "precision bombing." It was so accurate and advanced that its mechanism was a military secret of the highest order. To keep one from being taken intact by the enemy, every bombsight was equipped with a small explosive charge that the bombardier was ordered to detonate in the event of a crash landing in any unknown or foreign territory.

When the bombsight's cross hairs were properly synchronized, it had a margin of error on the ground—the "coefficient of cross-trail"—of fifty feet. Because the plane's bomb-release mechanism was timed so that the bombs hit the ground at fifty-foot intervals, for a single plane the coefficient of cross-trail was, as a practical matter, zero (absent the effect of exploding flak). In addition, Marauders flew in squadrons of six flights, and each flight was composed of six planes in tight formation. The wing airplanes in each flight were ordered to drop their bombs simultaneously with the lead aircraft. The chance of missing a target was remote. Once a bomb hit a pier, a built-in three- or four-second delay allowed it to penetrate the pier before exploding. We could always destroy the piers.

The six flights engaged in a mission assembled over the "initial point," some thirty or forty miles from the target.

The lead flight of six planes would usually approach the target directly from that point. The next would veer forty-five degrees to the right, then move toward the target from that direction. The third would veer forty-five degrees to the left before turning toward the target. The subsequent sets of six airplanes would follow a similar pattern. These multidirectional approaches were designed to confuse the radar-directed antiaircraft gunners. The planes did not collide over the target because they would approach the target at slightly different altitudes. In any case, "bombs away" would occur about a half mile short of the target. The thrust from the motion of the plane propelled the bomb forward as much as the force of gravity pulled it downward. Both forces acting together created the bomb's trajectory toward the target.

Each squadron would engage in evasive action by changing direction frequently. Again, these maneuvers were designed to create an ever-changing target for the anti-aircraft gunners below. At about thirty seconds before an estimated "bombs away" the automatic pilot was activated, and at that point the bombardier controlled the airplane with the bombsight.

The airplane then moved "on course" straight toward the target. The bombsight's vertical cross hair (stabilized by a horizontal gyroscope) adjusted the plane's heading to compensate for wind direction and speed; the horizontal cross hair (stabilized by the vertical gyroscope) timed the distance from the target that the bomb would be released. The bombsight itself released the bombs at the exact time required and, by a radio connection, simultaneously released the bombs in the wing ships. A bomb run took about thirty seconds from "on course" until bombs away. It also took just about thirty seconds for antiaircraft shells to reach the airplane's altitude, although the antiaircraft gunners estimated the targeted plane's course while it was still flying evasively.

Those thirty seconds of the bomb run were the most dangerous for American fliers over Europe. The bombardier in the Plexiglas nose was perhaps the most vulnerable. I remember too clearly and painfully another mission, when I briefed a bombardier who had never flown a combat mission about how to read the aerial photographs of the target. On the bomb run his plane received a direct hit, the flak shell exploded, and all hands were killed.

My plane was always our squadron's lead Marauder in France. On this bombing run our plane was badly shot up. Most significantly, its radio system was knocked out. The airplane had self-sealing gas tanks, and though they had been shot through and undoubtedly lost some fuel they did not explode. There may have been damage to the hydraulic system as well. But none of the crew was injured.

At bombs away the pilot, Herb Christiansen, took control, turned sharply to the left and dropped two thousand feet, increasing the airspeed from about 190 miles per hour (slow by today's standards) to 220 or 230 miles per hour. The turn, the drop in altitude, and the increased speed were intended to throw off the antiaircraft gunners. But at that moment it seemed that the heavens opened up, as hail, sleet, and high winds engulfed us. The formation of six airplanes could no longer be maintained. Each had to fend for itself. The world disappeared in fog, snow, sleet, and darkness.

Probably a thousand planes were scrambling over Europe to find landing strips. Some crews bailed out. One perhaps apocryphal story reports that an airman who bailed out lost his harness as the parachute jerked open. But the parachute caught his pants pocket on the strap clasp, and he was wafted upside down all the way to the ground. Just as he was about to hit it, a high wind pulled him sideways and landed him gently in a meadow.

If our pilot had had radio contact or if I could have navigated based on ground observation, the destruction of the bomber and bombsight would not have occurred. But precise navigation was impossible. There was no way of estimating the wind direction and speed and no visible or recognizable checkpoints on the ground.

Heading generally west from the target area, in time we saw a ghostly glow—apparently the lights of Paris diffused by the clouds. While cities around the world from New York to Moscow were blacked out every night, Paris had become a mutually agreed open city, truly the City of Light—and it had been liberated in August.

I plotted a course from what I judged was the northern margin of Paris, but since it was based on a fog-diffused glow I knew it was only an educated guess. One apparent landing strip turned out to be the main street of a town. After far more time than it would have taken to fly from Paris to our field, I spotted a landing strip. Gasoline was surely getting low, although we could not be sure how low as it was not measured by a gauge but by engine time and we knew we had lost some fuel. Christiansen buzzed the field to let the tower know he needed to land. The tower must have guessed that our radio was out and sent up flares from the tower, which was near the upwind end of the runway. Christiansen and copilot Don Haas assumed the flares were at the downwind end of the runway and that they should land from that direction. There was no way of knowing the wind direction or speed at an unknown airfield in total darkness. This was a crucial decision.

The B-26 Marauder was heavily armored, bristling with .50-caliber machine guns, and designed with short wings to permit higher speed. It had the highest wing loading of any military airplane, helping to give it a superb record in combat. But it would "stall"—drop like a stone—when its airspeed fell below about 150 miles per hour. Normal commercial aircraft of that day could remain airborne at 75 or 80 miles per hour. The high speed needed to fly a B-26 Marauder caused it to be affectionately named the "flying brick" or even the "flying coffin."

If the tailwind was, say, 35 miles per hour, and the plane landed downwind, the speed over the runway would have been 215 miles per hour. At that speed it would have eaten up the runway before it landed. In the high wind that day, it was vital to land upwind. But the fliers—pilot, copilot, and I—were in the dark.

I left the glass nose for the navigation desk behind the pilots and, after checking, called out, "Wheels down and locked."

A few moments later Christiansen called out, "Down, you son-of-a-bitch, down!" The plane hit the runway hard, the landing gear folding and the left wing scraping the runway. The copilot cut all electrical switches to avoid fire. The almost-empty gas tanks in the wings contained a lethal mixture of gasoline vapor and air. The left wing could have exploded like a bomb. We might have been making a groundspeed of 215. But the tanks held and we scraped to a stop.

The pilots left through the hatch over their seats. The enlisted men—engineer, radioman, and tail gunner—must have left through the top turret. I cannot remember whether I went forward to blow up the bombsight with the small charge under it, or whether it was smashed in the crash landing. I climbed through the hatch in the cockpit and, in the darkness, forgot that the wheels had folded up as

I braced for a sixteen-foot drop. Instead, after an unexpectedly short drop, I hit the ground with a thump, and, fearing a fire or worse, raced away from the plane.

We three officers—pilot, copilot, and bombardier-navigator—were immediately placed under house arrest. We had landed on an American fighter field.

We were baffled. We had held to a bomb run through a sky filled with flak. Each exploding shell from German antiaircraft guns looked like an inkblot in the air throwing out an expanding sphere of steel particles. Occasionally one came so close we could smell the burning powder. Our plane had been perforated by flak, the radio knocked out, the hydraulic lines in the tail turret spewing icy fluid. And we had destroyed the target. Then, in the pitch darkness with high wind and hail we finally found an airfield, and its tower sent up flares at the wrong end of the runway so that we made a crash landing that could have ended in an explosion.

And here we were under arrest.

After seeing that the enlisted men were taken care of, the officers were allowed a drink in the officers' club and dinner in the mess. A day or so later we were charged with destroying government property—the airplane and bombsight. After consulting among ourselves we arranged to radio the 386th Bomb Group and ask the squadron flight engineer to come to the fighter field, examine the airplane, and testify at the court-martial.

The court of high officers assembled. Each of the crew's officers testified to the events on the mission. We had counted the flak holes and reported the result: as I recall, 147 holes from the nose to the trailing edge of the wing. I remember testifying that if anyone should be court-martialed it should be the person who sent up flares upwind of the runway. The squadron engineer testified that he had drawn only a helmet full of gas from each tank (though he might have committed perjury in exaggeration). The verdict of acquittal took a few minutes.

Why were we court-martialed? Surely every aircraft's loss did not prompt such a proceeding. After I became a lawyer an explanation came to mind: Perhaps it was because some higher-up in the chain of command wanted to clear the slate—to have a trial regarding this incident and preclude any further prosecution.

13

Battle of the Bulge

France, 1944–1945

ON DECEMBER 16, 1944, a supercooled mist descended over northern Europe. It did not clear until December 21. Hitler had taken personal control of the German army in the west, relieving General Erwin Rommel of his command. Fourteen divisions were secretly moved south to the weak, lightly defended center of the Allied forces. How and why American intelligence failed to spot the troop movement is a mystery. A division is normally composed of fifteen thousand men. Fourteen divisions was a large army of soldiers.

John Willard Toland vividly tells the story in *Battle: The Story of the Bulge*. He had spent fifteen years interviewing everyone he could find who participated in the battle and survived, from General Eisenhower down to the lowest-ranking soldiers.

The story is how a terrible losing battle was turned into a victory—but not by generals who failed to take obvious precautions to reinforce the center held by green troops and had failed to spot the movement of fourteen German divisions. The battle was won by ordinary GIs fighting in a dense supercooled fog against seasoned German soldiers, many of whom were wearing American uniforms. When the Allies won that battle, they won the war in Europe. Had Hitler's army broken through and reached Antwerp, through which four American armies and one British army were supplied, the war would have lasted many more months or longer.

It is significant that the battle was fought amid a super-cooled fog. If you put a glass of distilled water in your freezer (and avoid even a slight tremor), the temperature of the water will fall below freezing, but the water will not turn to ice. If you shake it or it touches metal, it will immediately freeze into a solid. Mist is distilled water and, if supercooled, will turn to ice as soon as it touches metal. The GIs on our base near Beaumont-sur-Oise tried to remove the ice from the planes during the Battle of the Bulge but to no avail. Think of how the guns, helmets, and other equipment of the GIs fighting on the ground became encased in ice.

This is the story of my small and lucky part in this decisive battle against Hitler. My crew and I from time to time visited a nearby chateau which had wings set at an angle and a glass tower at the vertex. The tower housed a bedroom, where I would sleep for a couple of nights after the war was over. The family of a newspaperman who had fought in the French Underground during the Nazi occupation owned and lived in one wing of the chateau, while eighty war orphans lived in the other wing, cared for by the family's two daughters. We would take cigarettes to the family; they would give us fresh eggs. The family invited us for Christmas dinner. They were going to butcher a sheep for the meal.

That Christmas dinner never happened. There is no institution more helpless or vulnerable than an airbase in weather that freezes the planes to the ground. The following events occurred from December 16 to 21, 1944, on our base and on Army Air Force bases all over northern Europe. We had been advised that the Germans had launched a major attack and we received orders to fly west until we found a base with sufficient visibility to permit landing. We were highly concerned about the attack, but it was impossible to carry out that order. The planes were covered with ice.

The officers whiled away time in the officers' club. In fact, we invited our enlisted crew to drink in the club with us (fraternization normally being prohibited). One GI dug a foxhole, a futile effort to do something useful. I was walking toward the officers' club with Jim O'Kelly, our radio operator, a staff sergeant. He looked down the hole and called to the GI who was digging, "Deep hole, ain't it?" Most of us thought if we were going to be blown up, it would be better in a warm tent with a fire of lubricating oil than in a cold foxhole. At some point, radio contact with Bomber Command and air force headquarters was cut off. We suspected that there was probably a fifth column in the woods near the base, but we could do nothing about it.

When the weather warmed up enough to melt the ice on the planes, two disastrous explosions occurred as one plane and then another was about to take off. The wire connections to the ailerons had been filed by saboteurs and failed under the pressure of a 150-miles-per-hour takeoff. The crews were killed in the explosions of full loads of 500-pound demolition bombs. All planes then had to be inspected and repaired.

On Christmas Day, we were briefed for a mission to bomb a railroad bridge at Konz Karthaus. The mission was constantly delayed owing to weather, but finally took off. Then, a second mission flew to bomb the Keuchingen railroad bridge and returned to a cold Christmas dinner at the officers' mess.

Between December 23 and February 2, we bombed fourteen railroad bridges, one highway, and one railroad junction. Often a bridge destroyed on one day had to be bombed again a day or two later because the Germans had rebuilt it. These bridges, junctions, and highways were the main supply route for the German army, as well as its exit route from the Bulge back to the Rhine River.

I believe that destruction of the bridges and roads by our medium bombers' accurate bombing must have made a major contribution to the victory of the Battle of the Bulge.

14

A Second Court-Martial

France, 1945

AFTER A MISSION briefing and as the bombers' engines were revving up to taxi toward the runway, one bombardier-navigator in our squadron decided he was not going to fly anymore. He dropped through the bomb-bay doors and walked forward under the fuselage, between the spinning props, back to his tent. The mission took off with thirty-five instead of thirty-six airplanes. Bomber Command wanted to know why and ordered a court-martial.

Captain Keating, the flight surgeon, was prepared to give the bombardier-navigator a medical leave for a few weeks in London until he recovered. He was obviously seriously emotionally disturbed. He refused, stated he would not fly another military mission under any circumstance, and asked for a court-martial. He asked me (I had been through the court-martial following the crash landing) to represent him in his court-martial. I was not a lawyer then, and this was a capital offense; the defendant needed a competent professional lawyer. I told Colonel Corbin, the group commanding officer, that unless I received a direct order to the contrary I would not represent the defendant.

The defendant was given an effective lawyer from the judge advocate general's office, who made the case for emotional instability or temporary insanity, but the court brushed it off. With a million men in mortal combat on the western front, the court could not signal that there was a ready way out from duty in the skies over Europe. The defendant was sentenced to ten years in Leavenworth prison. Perhaps it was the plea of emotional instability that motivated the court to limit the sentence to a jail term. The sentence did not sit well at SHAEF, and the court-martial judges received a reprimand from General Eisenhower.

After the war, the sentence was reduced to two years. The officer, according to reliable rumors, later married a South American heiress and lived, so far as is known, happily ever after.

15

A Lost Airplane and War's End

From France to Vermont, *1945*

WE SPENT THE MONTHS between the end of the war in Europe and going home exploring France and Germany by air. Among our explorations was a visit to my younger brother, Billy, who had been wounded by a shell in the Battle of the Bulge and was confined to a hospital bed in the south of France. I could speak German and learned that a prisoner who had been an SS trooper was administering penicillin injections to wounded soldiers in that hospital. I was shocked and I reported that to the colonel in charge of the hospital, a physician, strongly suggesting that the prisoner be taken off that duty. The colonel also was shocked at this information and said he would take action.

Incidentally, though our army was totally segregated at the time, hospital wards were not; white and black soldiers mixed without incident.

Having recently read Henry Adams's classic *Mont-Saint Michel and Chartres*, I also flew over that fabled island monastery to view it from the air. It was an awesome sight: There was only a tidal causeway and at high tide the monument was an island—not connected to the mainland as it is today.

At long last, toward the end of July, I received two sets of orders, one open and one sealed. The open orders were to return to the States—to fly from strip A-74 in Cambrai, France, to Hunter Field, Savannah, Georgia, thence to the Charleston Point of Embarkation staging area. I was to navigate a flight of six airplanes back to the United States in several stages: via Marseilles and Casablanca to Dakar on the West Coast of Africa; thence across the South Atlantic to Fortaleza, Brazil; then by stages via Venezuela to San Juan, Puerto Rico; and finally to an airfield in South Carolina, where I would be released for three weeks of RR&R (rest, recovery, and recuperation). I was then to open the sealed orders.

At Dakar we were carefully briefed prior to our transoceanic flight, particularly with respect to a two-hundred-mile weather pattern, the "equatorial front." It was always there somewhere near the Equator—sometimes a little north of it, sometimes a little south—but always a meteorological factor to be reckoned with, a vast cloud bank containing dangerous turbulence. The bomb bays had been fitted with large auxiliary fuel tanks, but even so there was barely enough fuel for a nine-hour flight. If the planes were off course by as much as one degree, they would sight land too far off to reach the Fortaleza airfield. No pilot could maintain a course to within one degree for nine hours. As bombardier-navigator, I kept a running record of the compass headings to be certain that our off-course deviations balanced out, and if they didn't I told the pilot what corrections to make.

When we approached the equatorial front, I ordered the wing planes on the right wing to turn thirty degrees off course to the right for thirty seconds, and those on the left wing to make a similar left turn, fly for thirty seconds, and then turn on course again. The plane directly behind was ordered to drop altitude one thousand feet to avoid hitting the lead plane. The planes were flying at about 180 miles per hour. The thirty seconds of flying time would carry each plane about one and a half miles off the original course, well within easy sight of the lead plane when they came out of the front. During the flight through the front, I kept an especially meticulous record of headings because the frontal air was so turbulent. There was supposed to be a barge west of the front sending a radio signal to confirm our position, but we never saw the barge or made radio contact. No matter, it was vital to maintain the dead-reckoning navigational record. To search for the barge would have wasted fuel and could have ended in disaster.

After an hour or more of flying through the equatorial front, five planes emerged. The sixth was nowhere to be seen, but was contacted by radio. The pilot thought his turn to the right was more than thirty degrees, though he didn't remember by how much, and he stayed on that course for more than thirty seconds, but he did not know how much longer. Given the limited amount of fuel, this was a dangerous condition. I gave him a gradual correction back toward the formation of the five visible airplanes; too sharp a correction and the lost plane might cross our path unseen either ahead of or behind us and been lost. An hour or so after leaving the front, we spotted the lost plane coming toward us from the north.

About nine hours from Dakar, we sighted land some twenty minutes flying time north of the Fortaleza airport. There were no international protocols then and each airport spoke its own language. The pilot had to land "on the beam"—a directional radio signal—there being no verbal communication because none of us spoke Portuguese. We spent a day there before continuing on in stages toward Puerto Rico. When we approached San Juan, we learned from radio stations broadcasting in English that a day or two earlier—on August 15, 1945—Japan had surrendered after atomic bombs were dropped on the cities of Hiroshima and Nagasaki. The war was over.

At the airfield in South Carolina, after leaving my crew, I telephoned my wife, who was living in her family's farmhouse in Putney, Vermont. Boarding a train for Fort Dix, New Jersey, I shared a compartment with a colonel who was bemoaning the end of the war because it meant a reduction in rank for him to captain. At Fort Dix I asked to be discharged from the army. The captain in charge asked to see my 101 file. After studying it for a few minutes, he looked up and said, "Would five o'clock this afternoon be soon enough, Lieutenant?" He actually made it by six.

I was compelled to agree to enter the reserves for five years, then I was discharged. I surrendered my sealed orders, which were issued before the war in the Pacific had ended, and was on my way to Vermont to see Marion for the first time in over a year. The sealed orders, which were to be opened after sixty days of RR&R, probably ordered me to report to an airfield somewhere, become part of a new crew, and proceed to the Far East.

PART THREE

A Young Lawyer

16

How We Taught History

Putney, Vermont, 1945–1946

THE FOUNDER AND DIRECTOR of the Putney School, Carmelita Hinton, offered me the chance to teach American and medieval history. This was, I believe, because Marion was a graduate of the school, and Carmelita knew her well.

In planning my courses, I wanted to avoid certain elements of the conventional teaching of history—principally the use of a textbook. A textbook taught students that history was what happened in the book, that what happened had to happen the way it happened, and that it always happened for the best. Textbooks in those days usually had many pictures and black-type subject headings. They were almost designed to stop a student from thinking. Students learned what was in the book and fed it back to teachers in examinations.

The textbook I had at the Ethical Culture Fieldston School—David Saville Muzzey's *History of the American People*—was as boring a book as could be found. It described the Civil War as if slavery had nothing to do with it. The Civil War, Muzzey wrote, was fought "to preserve the Union," probably because the book was sold to high schools throughout the Southern states. Most courses at Fieldston were excellent and some outstanding, such as Elbert Lenrow's great books seminar and Zelda Colvin's senior mathematics course. American history was an exception.

I taught my courses at the Putney School through the examination of issues, usually ethical and pragmatic issues. A student would write a paper on some question, copies were made for the rest of the class to read, and we would discuss the issue in class. I urged students to discuss the issues from the point of view of the time when the question arose, rather than by basing their judgments on the moral criteria of today. Often students took sides on the issues.

For example, in the twelfth century there was a debate across Europe as to whether in the ceremony of Mass the sacramental bread and wine actually turned into the flesh and blood of Jesus. I asked one student to take one side of the issue and another to take the other, then to go to the library and build their arguments. The approach was similar in American history. After the papers were written and distributed, we discussed the issue at hand.

The students enjoyed these classes, as did I, and as often as not there was no right answer to the issue under discussion. Some sixty-odd years later, I was especially pleased when one of my former students chanced to meet our daughter, Ellen, at the memorial service for Jack Langstaff, director of the annual theatrical productions the *Christmas Revels* and *Spring Revels* in Washington, Boston, and New York City. My former student told her my class had not only changed his thinking about history, but actually affected his view of life.

I have thought about those two courses taught so many years ago by a young, brash teacher, just home from fighting in a war that itself had complex moral issues—particularly the use of nuclear weapons. The bomb brought the war to an end, permitted me to go home, and permitted Marion and me to begin our life together. The question that President Harry Truman was compelled to answer when he suddenly became president upon FDR's death was whether to drop the atomic bomb on two Japanese cities. It was a terrible weapon.

We had by then virtually destroyed the Japanese air force and navy. But Japan had five million well-trained men under arms. We had hardly touched this huge army, which would fight to the last man to save their island from invasion just as the British under Churchill would have fought to preserve their island nation. (And just as the indigenous people of Okinawa had fought fiercely.) General George C. Marshall estimated that one million American soldiers and many more Japanese would be killed if we had to invade Japan, and the war would go on for several years. I do not say Truman made the right decision or the wrong decision, only that it was a painful decision to make. It is the kind of decision the president alone can make, leaving him all alone in the making of it. How would my students decide Truman's issue?

17

Murder: Trials of a Young Lawyer

New York and Washington, 1950

BEFORE I WAS ASSIGNED a case to try on my own in private law practice at Paul, Weiss, Rifkind, Wharton & Garrison, I worked on only two cases, one of them a libel case under Sam Silverman, who was one of the firm's litigation partners and later a justice on the Appellate Division of the New York State Supreme Court. In the second case, I assisted another partner, Simon H. Rifkind, in trying a securities fraud matter.

The libel case arose because the newspaper *PM* called a lawyer named Klein a "Jew-baiting Jew" under a gruesome cartoon. *PM* was reporting on a sedition trial of some thirty Nazi sympathizers that had occurred during World War II in Washington, D.C. Klein defended one of them, an American colonel who had moved around Eastern Europe during the interwar period publishing anti-Semitic Nazi filth. In his opening statement to the jury, Klein had not argued that those anti-Semitic views were protected speech under the First Amendment, but rather had adopted his client's substantive opinions. This defense had prompted *PM*'s harsh characterization.

PM, a short-lived liberal New York daily, was owned outright by the banker and department store heir Marshall Field. Klein sued Field personally since he owned the newspaper in his own name in order to claim income-tax deductions for the operating losses. We were defending Field. I spent hours in the library of the Anti-Defamation League locating the colonel's rantings against Jews and the Sanhedrin as well as his other invective.

The foreman of the jury was a man with a heavy German accent who lived in the Yorkville section of Manhattan, an old German neighborhood and center of German sympathizers. But one member of the jury was a newspaper reporter and another was an advertising writer. Sam hoped that in addition to those two we could pick up at least a third juror, enough under New York law in civil cases to prevent a verdict against Marshall Field.

The jury was out for seven hours, we thought possibly calculating damages for the libel. In the end we were startled by a unanimous verdict for Marshall Field. Afterward, I collared the foreman, who said they had taken about ten minutes to reach a 10–2 verdict in our favor, but he, the foreman, had insisted that they bring back a unanimous verdict. The two holdouts had been the two writers! I learned from this that it is impossible to predict how a juror will vote based upon his or her occupation or manner. The endless effort of lawyers to pick a favorable jury is largely wasted time.

The securities fraud case in which I assisted Judge Rifkind (his title dated from years on the Federal District Court) raised doubts in my mind about one of the core elements of our the criminal justice system: the use of grand juries. We were representing a broker who was a minor accomplice in the fraud (if there had been a fraud). The principal person accused of fraud had been convicted of draft dodging during the war. He spoke with a foreign accent, and even aside from those characteristics would otherwise have been unpopular with an American jury. Isidor Kressel, a highly competent lawyer, represented him. Kressel spoke in an extremely soft voice. You could hear a whisper in the courtroom when he was asking questions or addressing the jury.

Grand jury minutes were secret then, except under narrow circumstances, but we suspected that a transcript of the Securities and Exchange Commission (SEC) fraud investigation was the principal evidence on which the grand jury had based its indictment. I suggested that we move under Rule 6 of the Federal Rules of Criminal Procedure to obtain the transcript of the SEC investigation. Rule 6 provided that the defendant in a criminal case could obtain "documents" from the prosecutor or a third party in advance of trial. It probably referred to documents such as contracts, letters, memorandums, and the like. We nevertheless argued that the transcript was a "document" even though it may have run to thousands of pages with many attached exhibits. Judge Rifkind made a brilliant argument before Judge Sidney Sugarman in the U.S. District Court for the Southern District of New York and obtained an order requiring the SEC to produce the transcript.

The SEC was furious. It placed the transcript in possession of a clerk in its New York City office who was instructed to refuse to obey the order. Judge Sugarman committed the clerk to prison for contempt of court, and the SEC filed an appeal from the contempt order in the court of appeals.

I was dispatched to Washington to discuss the appeal with an assistant general counsel of the SEC. I showed him a number of cases holding that before final judgment, the only issue on appeal from a contempt order was whether the district judge had jurisdiction to issue the order, which Judge Sugarman clearly had. The SEC lawyer recognized the rule immediately. The commission dismissed the indictment against our client rather than disclose the transcript of its investigation.

Although we had resolved the problem in this case, I drew from it the lesson that a grand jury could be an instrument of oppression in a criminal case. It could develop evidence in secret by issuing subpoenas to produce documents and by taking secret testimony of witnesses, while the defendant had extremely limited rights of discovery. The defendant might be surprised at the trial by evidence he had had no knowledge of and no prior opportunity to controvert. It was as if the criminal procedure created a game rather than a framework for a sincere effort to arrive at the truth.

My own first case involved the Brown Paper Company. Brown manufactured paper from pulp logs grown in Maine, New Hampshire, and Vermont. It marketed its paper through an agent in New York City who sold the company's paper in the mid-Atlantic region, comprising Connecticut, New York, New Jersey, and Pennsylvania. The agent also represented a dozen other companies selling various products not competitive with Brown Paper. A plaintiff, whose name I have long since forgotten, claimed that he had, in fact, invented one of the Brown Paper Company's papers.

Beginning in about 1920 this person had been repeatedly claiming payments for his invention, but the Brown Paper Company denied that the product was his invention and denied any compensation for manufacturing and selling it. In 1950 or 1951 the individual brought suit against the company in the New York State Supreme Court, stating his claim as the inventor of one of their papers. The company retained Paul, Weiss, Rifkind, Wharton & Garrison to defend its position. The firm turned the case over to me, one of the newest associates.

As I looked at the case I recognized that if there were a claim, it had arisen some thirty years earlier. The statute of limitations would long ago have barred the claim, except that under the law of New York the statute is suspended during periods that the state courts lacked jurisdiction. This usually happens when the defendant is living in another state, or travels abroad, or is, as they say, "on the lam."

The question here was whether the Brown Paper Company had a sufficient "presence" in New York through its selling agent so as to give the courts of New York jurisdiction. The company had been doing business in this manner for some thirty years. If there was jurisdiction, the claim was barred by the statute of limitations. If jurisdiction failed for want of a presence in New York, the claimant had to sue in New Hampshire. I made a motion to dismiss the action, for want of jurisdiction or as barred by the statute of limitations. It was a motion I could not lose.

Counsel for the claimant asked me to consent to several extensions of time to respond to the motion, to which I readily agreed. Then one day he called me and said, in a bitter voice, "I know that a corporation has neither an ass to be kicked or a soul to be damned, but your client murdered my client, who, when I explained your motion to him, jumped out of the window and killed himself." He then hung up the phone.

This revelation caused me deep distress. My hands began to shake. It was, after all, the first case I had ever handled by myself, with no supervision. After I regained my composure I called the lawyer back.

"My client didn't even know I made that motion," I said. "If anyone killed your client it was I, but in my opinion he killed himself." And I hung up. I reported the conversation to Sam Silverman, who agreed with my motion and my response to the lawyer's charge.

Some twenty or more years later I came to know Fletcher Brown, a scion of the Brown Paper Company family, who had married a good friend of Marion's and mine. We visited Charlotte and Fletcher occasionally during summers at Charlotte's house in Maine. They were astonished and shocked by the story.

The Sumner Tunnel and *Moby Dick*

Cambridge and Long Island, 1950–1951

IN THE AUTUMN OF 1950 Marion and I found ourselves in Cambridge. Marion was pregnant with Kate, and suddenly felt she was having a miscarriage. I took her to Women's Hospital where she was examined and released to drive home at slow speed and no bumps. I had to go through Sumner Tunnel, which in those days had a cobblestone road. I drove through the tunnel at a speed of 10 miles per hour. All the cars behind me were honking their horns constantly. I could not explain to them the reason that I was driving so slowly or they might have sympathized with me. I was determined. We got through without mishap and drove slowly back to Howard King's house on Long Island, where we were staying.

It was several months until Marion was due and during those months she was confined to bed. We read *Moby Dick* aloud to each other and finally on January 11, 1951, Marion started labor and in due course a healthy Kate was born at New York Hospital.

Joe McCarthy, Harold Stassen and Me

Washington, 1953

JOSEPH RAYMOND McCARTHY—like Charles Boycott, the Earl of Sandwich, Charles Ponzi, Benedict Arnold, and Vyacheslav Molotov—gave his name to the English language. "McCarthyism," coined in 1950, speaks frighteningly of McCarthy's demagogic and unsubstantiated accusations, and his attacks on the character or patriotism of opponents.

McCarthy ran for the U.S. Senate in 1946, defeating Robert M. La Follette Jr., the Progressive Party senator from Wisconsin. It is a puzzle that the people of Wisconsin could have replaced a noble senator who fought for progressive causes with a hard-right candidate like McCarthy, although McCarthy's propensity for unsubstantiated attacks did not become evident until several years later. Even after his demagoguery echoed throughout the nation, Wisconsin reelected him in 1952.

In 1950 McCarthy suddenly rose to national notoriety when he asserted in a speech in Wheeling, West Virginia, that he had a list of "eighty-one" (the number kept changing) members of the Communist Party who were employed in the State Department.

McCarthy was never able to produce a shred of evidence to support his charges. In later years, in addition to the State Department, McCarthy made accusations of Communist infiltration into the administration of President Truman, the Voice of America, and the United States Army. He even charged General George C. Marshall, President Eisenhower's mentor, with treason for having "lost" China. McCarthy also used charges of Communism, Communist sympathies, or disloyalty to attack politicians and individuals in private life. In the Army-McCarthy hearings of 1954, the counsel for the army, Joseph Welch, created a phrase that resonated throughout the nation, "Have you no sense of decency, sir?"

After those hearings, support for McCarthy began to fade. Later in 1954, the Senate, on a motion by Ralph Flanders, Republican from Vermont, voted 67 to 22 to censure McCarthy for attacking another senator. If the censure motion had been for attacking the many innocent victims of McCarthy's baseless attacks, it is possible that Flanders could not have attracted the Republican votes needed to pass the motion.

The only Democrat who did not support the resolution, Senator John F. Kennedy, was in the hospital recovering from back surgery. He never stated how he would have voted. His younger brother, Robert F. Kennedy, was minority counsel to McCarthy's committee; his father was a friend of

McCarthy and invited him frequently to the family compound on Cape Cod. Kennedy was once heard to remark that many of his constituents supported McCarthy.

The actions of the Foreign Operations Administration (FOA) in supplying grain to the Soviets were the subject of one McCarthy committee investigation. The committee had notified the FOA on a Friday that it would hold hearings the following Monday. The director of the FOA at the time was Harold Stassen, a liberal Republican, former governor of Minnesota, and later a perennial Republican candidate for president. Given such short notice for the hearing, he was, understandably, totally unprepared.

The law firm where I was then a young associate— Radnor, Zito, Kominers & Fort—represented some companies in which the Greek shipping tycoon Aristotle Onassis had a significant interest. Those companies were engaged in carrying bulk grain from the United States to the Soviet Union, and the cargoes were financed by the FOA. I was sent down to attend the hearings and report.

Stassen had played a key role in the 1952 Republican nominating convention when he released his delegates to Dwight Eisenhower, thus helping him to defeat Ohio Senator Robert Taft on the first ballot. Stassen served in the Eisenhower administration, filling posts that included director of the Mutual Security Administration and special assistant to the president for disarmament matters.

During this period, Stassen held cabinet rank. He led a quixotic effort, perhaps covertly encouraged by Eisenhower, who may have had serious reservations about Vice President Richard Nixon's qualifications for the presidency, to "dump Nixon" at the 1956 Republican National Convention.

At the hearing on financing grain shipments to the Soviet Union, McCarthy attacked Stassen in his customary fashion. Neither Stassen nor his general counsel were able to defend themselves.

I began to boil at the baseless attacks and the inept defense. Finally I rose, came to the front of the hearing room, and called out: "Mr. Chairman, Mr. Chairman, if the committee is interested in the facts, the United States government is daily paying large amounts of subsidies to at least four American shipping companies to transport to the Soviet Union all manner of general property used by a modern civilization." I was referring to American President Lines, United States Lines, Lykes Lines and Pacific Far East Lines.

Whereupon, the chairman ordered the marshal to remove me from the hearing. I was promptly lifted up by the guards and removed from the hearing room. Plainly, the committee was not interested in the facts. No legislation or administrative action was taken responsive to those hearings.

I wondered whether I would keep my job, but the firm was delighted.

20

Top Secret:
Cowardice in the State Department

Washington, 1951–1970

IN THE EARLY SUMMER OF 1950, about the time the Korean War broke out, Michael Cardozo, a nephew of Justice Benjamin Cardozo and an assistant legal adviser to the State Department, offered me a job in the Office of the Legal Adviser. I was to be the lawyer for Harry Truman's "Point Four" program, which the president had outlined in his 1949 inaugural address.

The president's first "point" was to provide unfaltering support for the United Nations, the second was to continue "programs for world economic recovery," the third was to support free nations against aggression, and the fourth was to "embark upon a bold new program for making the benefits of our scientific advances and industrial progress available for the improvement and growth of underdeveloped areas." I was delighted and excited at the prospect of being the lawyer for this valuable program.

While I waited for the necessary top-secret clearance, I continued working as an associate at Paul, Weiss, Rifkind,

Wharton & Garrison. And I arranged to rent a portion of a large house on Ordway Street in Washington, D.C., sharing it with a college and law school classmate, George Prince, and his wife, Kitty.

Months went by and I awaited the clearance. I called Mr. Cardozo almost every month, but each time was told that the persons working on security clearances were especially busy because of the Korean War. In time this excuse seemed less and less likely. There must be something wrong, I thought—something in my background causing the delay. Senator McCarthy was continuing his unpredictable and unsubstantiated attacks on the State Department and there was a near epidemic of political paranoia in the land. Could it be that I was somehow suspect for my membership (and leadership position) in the Harvard Liberal Union a decade before? But that group was formed by dissidents when the Harvard Student Union refused to condemn the Soviet invasion of Finland in 1939. Further, Eleanor Roosevelt had invited the officers of the Liberal Union to go to Washington and talk to President Roosevelt. Nevertheless something was stopping this clearance, so I decided to withdraw my application for the State Department position and seek employment with a private law firm.

Nineteen years later, at a reception for John D. J. Moore, the U.S. ambassador to Ireland, I met Mr. Cardozo for the second time and engaged him in conversation: "Mr. Cardozo, you may not remember me, but in 1950 you offered me a job in the legal adviser's office, subject to a top-secret clearance. I was to be the office's lawyer to President Truman's Point Four program."

"I do not remember you, Mr. Schlefer, but I remember the situation very clearly," he told me. "You would never have been cleared. Nor would we ever have denied you a clearance." The obstacle, as it turned out, was Carol Weiss King, Marion's aunt by marriage. Marion's uncle, Gordon King, who died in the 1930s, had been married to Carol. She was a lawyer who represented Communists and other fellow travelers. Mr. Cardozo explained, "Because of Carol Weiss King's relationship to you, the department was afraid that, if you were cleared, the Hearst press and the *Chicago Tribune* would have attacked it and asserted that McCarthy's charge of Communists in the State Department was true. On the other hand, if we had denied you a clearance, the *New York Times* and the *Washington Post* would have attacked the department for yielding to spurious charges." It was obvious that he had lied when he said that the delay was due to the Korean War.

"Of course, Mr. Cardozo, there was no professional relationship between me and Carol," I replied. "And inaction by the department had the effect of denying a clearance and yielding to Joe McCarthy's outrageous charges. The department had a lot of guts!"

Howard King, Marion's father and Carol's brother-in-law, was a distinguished engineer who had a top-secret clearance throughout the war. Carol's brother, Louis Weiss, was one of the founders of the important law firm that bore his name. An elegant lady, Carol was possibly sympathetic to Marxism. But she was not the one looking for a job in the State Department. Why would my wife's aunt by marriage have affected my being a security risk? The State Department's decision changed my life and the life of my family from what they would have been had the department been more courageous.

What was truly "top-secret" was the pusillanimous conduct of the State Department.

PART FOUR

An Advocate:
Principles and Practice

President of the Lawyers Alliance for World Security

21

Merrimack, Monitor and a Chief Justice

Delaware River, Philadelphia, and Washington, 1953–1954

WHEN WORLD WAR II ENDED, the United States Maritime Commission was the owner of a huge fleet composed of slow, small Liberty ships, faster and larger Victory ships, and many specialized ships including oil tankers. The creation and operation of this immense fleet was one of the miracles of the war. At one point we were dumping a Liberty ship into the water every four days, a fully complete seagoing cargo vessel. These oceangoing ships transported huge quantities of supplies across the world's oceans to our soldiers and those of our allies.

After the war the commission wanted to sell these ships to American citizens for documentation under the American flag and thus rebuild the U.S. Merchant Marine. Generally the commission took back a mortgage for 75 percent of the purchase price. This program was authorized by Congress in the Merchant Ship Sales Act of 1946.

Stavros Niarchos, a Greek national and international shipping magnate before the war, now needed new ships and the commission's fleet seemed a likely source—though not for a foreign national. Working with friends who were American citizens (of Greek origin or Greek descent), Niarchos lent them funds to form an American corporation and apply to purchase ships for documentation under the American flag. Since most of the stock was owned by American citizens, they represented that the corporation was an American citizen company. Two of the vessels purchased from the commission were the SS *Merrimack* and SS *Monitor*, T-2 oil tankers named after the famous Civil War ships and engaged in transporting crude oil from the Gulf of Mexico to refineries in New Jersey.

Some years later the Civil Division of the Justice Department, headed by Warren Burger, claimed the company that owned the two vessels was not a U.S. citizen corporation because Niarchos had loaned the money to the stockholders to buy their stock. The government argued that in reality Niarchos controlled the company; hence it was not an American citizen company and its ships were subject to forfeiture. As the company's counsel, I believed that the government's position was legally flawed; as a private citizen I felt its position was outrageous.

As the Merrimack sailed up the Delaware River in 1952, the marshal from the federal district court in New Jersey arrested the vessel, and the government filed a libel of forfeiture in that court. A "libel" is a term for instituting an admiralty proceeding, in this case to justify before the court the attaching or seizure of a vessel. Whitney North Seymour, a prominent New York lawyer, was able to persuade the judge to release the *Merrimack* on condition that the company furnish a bond. The judge was wrong. He was thinking of a customary suit in admiralty against a vessel for wages, collision damages, or supplies furnished to the ship, or for the cost of repairs and similar claims. The privilege of putting up a bond did not apply to forfeiture. A forfeiture normally applied to ships carrying drugs or other contraband, engaged in piracy, or engaged in a violation of sanctions. In such situations a bond was not permitted to release the vessel. The government did not want to release the *Merrimack*, because it wanted to force the company to acquiesce in the government's position. In this case where there was a genuine dispute over the claimed violation, forfeiture was clearly inequitable, and that inequity probably motivated the judge's decision.

The *Monitor* was the next vessel scheduled to sail up the Delaware River, and I as counsel was asked to board the vessel and direct the master to move the ship to the New Jersey side of the river so we could take advantage of the New Jersey judge's ruling in the *Merrimack* case. I had a little time before the vessel was due to arrive, which enabled me to research the jurisdiction of the New Jersey court. The statute creating the court provided that its jurisdiction extended to the boundary between Pennsylvania and New Jersey. The Coast and Geodetic Survey on its maps placed the boundary at the thread of the river (an imaginary line tracing the middle of a river). I asked for the survey's authority, causing some consternation, but in the end I found that it was based on a pre-American Revolutionary War treaty between the two colonies, which the Congress had later ratified. The treaty provided that the boundary was the thread of the river, but that the police power of Pennsylvania extended to mean high water on the New Jersey side. There was a possible issue here, but the judge in New Jersey had acted on the attachment by the court's marshal. And there was no other direct precedent.

On a Sunday morning, with snow falling on the river and the countryside in both states, the Monitor cleared quarantine near the mouth of the Delaware River. I chartered a launch, which took me out to the ship. The master had been advised of my arrival by radio and was awaiting me. A rope ladder was cast over the side for me to climb to the deck. By today's standards a T-2 tanker was a small ship. It could load 16,600 tons of crude oil. Some modern tankers can lift 400,000 tons of crude and many can lift from 60,000 to 160,000 tons. But as I climbed that rope ladder in the snow this T-2 tanker seemed immense. I thought I'd never get to the deck.

The master, at my instruction, hugged the New Jersey side of the river and discharged the ship's cargo into a tank farm in New Jersey. A lawyer from the Justice Department and a representative of the Maritime Administration approached the ship in a launch with the marshal from the federal district court in Pennsylvania. The master of the *Monitor* meanwhile was recording the proceedings on a reel-to-reel recorder, which he used whenever he disciplined a crew member so as to have a record in the event of a complaint by the crewman or his union. I advised the master to call down to the marshal that if he touched the ship, he would be sued on his bond because he was beyond the jurisdiction of his court and a mere trespasser. This worked.

The lawyer from the Justice Department asked me if I would appear in the Philadelphia court. We needed some help from the port of Philadelphia unless we sailed to another port where we would have again faced the Justice Department. A tanker emptied of its oil was a floating bomb, a lethal mixture of petroleum gas and air on the edge of a major city. The crew needed to be paid and released, garbage needed to be unloaded, and the master confronted other problems on arriving in port. I called down that I would appear provided he agreed that it would be a special appearance that enabled me to challenge the jurisdiction of the court. He readily agreed.

The Justice Department was able to get a judge into court on a Sunday morning. The judge was an old gentleman (though younger than I am today). The government wanted to argue the jurisdictional issue. I told the court I was not admitted to practice in Pennsylvania. The Justice lawyer immediately moved to admit me to practice for purposes of the case, and the court readily agreed. But the judge was not about to decide where the boundary of the Commonwealth of Pennsylvania lay that afternoon. He said we could present the issue to a judge of the court of appeals. I pointed out that we did not have an order from which to appeal. The judge didn't care and called Judge William H. Hastie, who came down to court on this snowy Sunday afternoon.

It was a rare privilege to sit in Judge Hastie's chambers and work out the problem presented by the predicament of the *Monitor*. He had been first in his class at Amherst; was a graduate of Harvard Law School, where he had been elected to the *Harvard Law Review;* had held distinguished positions under the Roosevelt administration; and was appointed to the U.S. Court of Appeals for the Third Circuit by President Truman—the first black court of appeals judge—and later appointed its chief judge.

I outlined the position of the parties including the government's claim on the citizenship issue. The statute provided that if an American-flag vessel was transferred by an American citizen to a noncitizen without the approval of the Maritime Administration, the vessel was forfeited to the government. I pointed out that the company could not have violated the statute, since only a transfer "by a citizen" could violate the statute and in this case the transfer was by the commission, not by a citizen, and in any event, I pointed out that the Maritime Commission must have approved what it actually did when it sold the vessel to the company. I also explained the holding of the district judge in New Jersey and that if the vessel were forfeited to the government before trial, incalculable harm would occur to the owner in the event it prevailed in the end.

Judge Hastie heard the government's legal argument that where there was a libel of forfeiture filed against a ship, the ordinary rule of posting bond for the ship's release did not apply. Judge Hastie then proposed that the ship post a bond for its release, and in addition that an agreement be negotiated between the parties for placing all the earnings of the ship during the litigation in an escrow account to abide the result of the litigation. The ship and its earnings would then be turned over to the prevailing party. The ship could be cleared of its dangerous gas, its garbage could be disposed of, the crew could be paid and dismissed, and other necessities could be carried out, all pending the negotiated agreement. But the company would be under a court order not to permit the ship to leave port before the escrow agreement had been negotiated and signed.

I called my client, Niarchos, in Paris and recommended that we accept Judge Hastie's proposal because, while we had all the equities, I feared the government was correct on the bond issue in a forfeiture case. In fact under Judge Hastie's proposal we obtained a bond. My client agreed. The government agreed. We both signed a short memorandum agreeing to Judge Hastie's proposal. In effect we had the result of the New Jersey court because we could post a bond.

The scene then shifted to the Justice Department in Washington, D.C., the office of Warren Burger, chief of the Civil Division and later chief justice of the United States. It was a case that made a name for him within the government and may even have had something to do with his appointment as chief justice. However, Morton Lifton, an able lawyer whom I had known from other contexts, conducted the actual negotiation on the government's side. Burger sat through and sometimes took part in the negotiations.

The document that emerged was much more intricate than the simple agreement Judge Hastie had described. Provisions had to be made for income taxes, for the possibility that once free from the restriction of Judge Hastie's order, the ship might escape from the reach of the government or the court. There were problems related to what would happen if the ship were sunk or damaged. Could repairs be made from the escrowed earnings without the government's approval? Suppose the owners wanted to charter the vessel to an affiliate, possibly earning substantial profits? Would these profits be deposited in the escrow account? How would potential criminal liability be handled?

This "Operating Stipulation," as we later called it, formed the pattern for agreements covering at least forty other ships claimed by the government. In my view these actions represented outrageous behavior on the part of the government. The commission had sold the vessels with full knowledge of the corporate and debt structure of the company, but now it claimed that that debt structure conferred control on Stavros Niarchos. When it sold the vessels it took back a mortgage for 75 percent of the value of the vessel, and under the mortgage was entitled to any financial information it wanted or needed. There was never an allegation of fraud by the company in the applications. And yet after selling the vessels and collecting the payment, the government moved to force the owners to forfeit the vessels.

In the end, the cases, at least for my clients, were settled by agreeing to build new vessels for American-flag operation. The only criminal case I knew of did not concern a company, but rather involved Niarchos himself. The charge was that he fraudulently misrepresented his control of various ship-owning companies. John Wilson, a lawyer experienced in criminal cases, tried it. I worked with him, and the jury returned a not-guilty verdict.

Many years later I met Chief Justice Burger at a Christmas party at the home of my friends Walter and Marie Ridder.

(Walter and Burger both came from Minnesota.) I happened to be standing next to him as we all were singing Christmas carols, and during a pause he said approximately this to me, "Mark, if I recommended you to President Reagan, I think he would appoint you to the Court of Appeals." I thanked him but said I was not interested in being a judge.

22

Ethics, Abe Fortas and John L. Lewis

Washington, 1955–1956

THIS INCIDENT CAN, in a sense, be seen as a conflict between two colossal figures: John L. Lewis, a giant in the American labor movement, and Abraham Fortas, a prominent lawyer later appointed to the U.S. Supreme Court. In another sense, the contest pitched 2.5 million Puerto Ricans against the ocean carrier that had served their needs for over seventy-five years.

Lewis, a powerful speaker and strategist, was the autocratic president of the United Mine Workers of America (UMW) and founder of the Congress of Industrial Organizations (CIO). He utilized the nation's dependence on coal to increase wages and improve mine safety. He supported technological improvements in mining even though that cost jobs, and these improvements enabled him to secure increases in wages and better working conditions for union members. A Republican, he was offered the job of Secretary of Labor under President Calvin Coolidge and rejected it. He supported Franklin D. Roosevelt for president in 1932 and 1936, but reverted to his Republican past and supported Wendell Willkie in 1940.

Lewis's adversary in this story, Abe Fortas, a founding partner of the law firm of Arnold, Fortas & Porter, was a complex person, a fine violist, and a man of charm who had served as lawyer in important pro bono cases. Fortas defended Clarence Earl Gideon, an indigent Floridian whose suit established the constitutional right of defendants to counsel in all serious criminal cases. Prior to Gideon the constitutional right to counsel had been limited to capital cases.

Fortas also represented the defendant in *Durham v. United States*, which overruled the existing McNaughten rule on insanity in criminal cases. Deriving from an 1843 case in the British House of Lords, the McNaughten rule had limited the insanity defense to situations where it could be shown that the defendant did not know right from wrong. This rule precluded modern psychiatric testimony to prove insanity. The Durham rule, allowing such testimony, is now settled law in the United States.

At about the same time, Fortas was found to have lied to a Senate committee and, while sitting on the Supreme Court, he accepted payments of $20,000 a year from a Wall Street financier, Louis Wolfson, who had hoped to have a criminal indictment reduced to a civil complaint. Wolfson was later convicted and sent to jail. Fortas was forced to resign from the Supreme Court, and the lawyers in the law firm he had cofounded would not accept him back.

Sometime around 1955 or 1956, John L. Lewis decided to form a company with other coal-mining interests to acquire American ships to transport coal to Europe. He planned to organize the seamen on the vessels. He thought that exporting coal to Europe would be feasible because an American miner could mine ten tons of coal a day, whereas a European miner could barely mine two tons a day. The technological improvements in American mining that Lewis had supported meant coal could literally be shipped to Newcastle—if freight rates allowed.

Three coal-related interests organized the American Coal Shipping Company. Lewis's United Mine Workers of America owned a one-third interest, three coal-carrying railroads (the Chesapeake & Ohio, the Norfolk & Western, and the Southern) together owned a one-third interest, and a group of coal-mining companies owned the final third. The president of American Coal was Walter Tuohy, also president of the Norfolk & Western Railway.

Lewis's plan for shipping coal to Europe was doomed to failure because a foreign-flag vessel with an Asian crew could carry coal to Europe for about four dollars a ton, while it would cost an American ship with an American-citizen crew sixteen dollars a ton. The efficiency of the American miner could not overcome the high cost of operating American-flag vessels. It took some time and a major investment before the three groups of owners bowed to this basic fact.

One of American Coal's first acts was to buy the A. H. Bull Steamship Company, an old-line American company whose history went back almost to the Civil War. At the time of the sale the company was still controlled by its founding family. The A. H. Bull company owned and operated a fleet of Liberty ships employed as tramps in the dry-bulk trades, largely grain cargoes under various economic development programs administered by the U.S. Agency for International Development (USAID). Dry-bulk cargoes are products like grain, fertilizer, coal, and iron ore that can be dumped unpackaged inside a ship's hold.

The law required that half of government-sponsored grain cargoes had to be shipped on American-flag vessels, regardless of labor cost; that law enabled these Liberty ships to compete for USAID cargoes. They would not have been able to compete commercially in the world market with low-cost foreign-flag vessels.

American Coal was particularly interested in the Liberty ships in the bulk trades because they were suitable for transporting coal. The company overlooked the fact that coal exported to Europe was not shipped under government-financed programs but had to compete in the world market with low-cost foreign-flag vessels.

The Bull Line also owned a fleet of common carrier liner-type cargo vessels, which served the trade between the Atlantic coast of the United States and Puerto Rico.

This trade, like those between the continental United States and Alaska or Hawaii, was reserved for American-flag ships. As the dominant common carrier in the Puerto Rican trade, offering twice-weekly service with large vessels at northern ports and weekly service at southern ports, Bull was the rate-making line. Its dock receipts for bagged raw sugar had passed as money during the Depression, when there was no other money in Puerto Rico. One could set one's clock by the departure of the Bull Lines ships. There was no need for warehousing in San Juan because the Bull vessel discharged her cargo precisely when local merchants needed the inventory.

In 1955, before the American Coal Shipping Company was organized, the Bull Lines, along with the other carriers in the Puerto Rico–U.S. trade, filed for a 15 percent general rate increase with the Federal Maritime Board, the government agency that regulated the rates in that trade. Abe Fortas represented the Commonwealth of Puerto Rico. He protested the rate increase on behalf of the commonwealth and asked the board to suspend the rate increase and order an investigation and public hearing. Although the increase was the first in the trade since World War II, the board ordered an investigation and public hearing but did not suspend the new rates, which went into effect immediately.

Shortly thereafter the American Coal Shipping Company bought all the stock of the A. H. Bull Steamship Company, the parent of the Bull Lines. The contest became deeper and more serious when, immediately after acquisition by American Coal, the Bull Lines filed a 10 percent additional general rate increase on top of the original 15 percent.

I represented the Bull Lines. I knew they desperately needed substantial additional revenue to survive. I also knew that the Bull Lines had made a serious mistake in failing to adjust rates in small amounts every few years after World War II, instead of waiting ten years to seek 26.5 percent increases in rates on all of the goods that the island's people needed to live.

The parties met with the board before the commonwealth's deadline for filing a protest against the second increase. Fortas demanded a suspension of the 10 percent increase. Having earlier anticipated and discussed the issue with Jim Light, the Bull Lines' traffic manager, I stated flatly that if the board suspended the Bull Lines' rate increase, the lines would immediately suspend service. That would have caused a catastrophe. It would take months for another carrier to free up adequate tonnage to fill in, and no carrier would even try under the then effective rates in the trade if the 10 percent increase were suspended. The island's 2.5 million people would somehow have to be fed and clothed. Fortas realized the seriousness of the consequences and suggested that the parties meet by themselves in a day or two. I agreed.

Before meeting with Fortas, the principals of American Coal and the Bull Lines met alone with me as their counsel. That meeting was at the Sheraton-Carlton (now the St. Regis) in Washington, D.C., where on almost any day around noon, one would see Mr. Lewis lunching alone at the same table in the dining room. The American Coal president, Walter Tuohy, asked Fred Heitman, the Bull Lines' vice president for finance, whether he knew where the Bull Lines would be financially in five years. Fred had no idea where the Bull Lines would be financially in five months, let alone five years. Lewis saw Fred's predicament and interjected, "Walter, I will tell you where every man, woman, and child in the United States will be five hundred years from now"—whereupon he proceeded to describe in Shakespearean rhythms and biblical cadences his vision of the nation in the remote future. A half hour later, having spent the time in rapt attention, everyone had forgotten Tuohy's question. The directors and officers of the two companies decided to listen to Fortas before reaching any decision.

At the next meeting, Fortas proposed a settlement of some modest sort—perhaps reducing the second increase to 7.5 percent or postponing it for a period. If they agreed, he offered assurances that the Commonwealth of Puerto Rico would not protest the increase. After some discussion, I asked Fortas what the commonwealth's position would be if the Federal Maritime Board on its own motion ordered an investigation. With a total increase in shipping costs of over 26 percent, I thought it was likely that the board would order an investigation, even if it decided not to suspend the increased rates. Fortas replied, "Well, in that case the commonwealth would have to oppose the increase."

Lewis stood up and responded in a deep resonant voice, "Where I come from, when we have a contract, we stand shoulder to shoulder to defend our contract." The meeting ended.

A few days later, Fred Heitman called me and said that Walter Tuohy had repeatedly tried to persuade the Bull Lines officers to withdraw the 10 percent general increase. He believed that Fortas was calling a client of his, Cyrus Eaton, to instruct Tuohy to persuade American Coal Shipping to tell the Bull Lines to withdraw the second rate increase.

A powerful figure, Eaton controlled several railroads including the Chesapeake & Ohio, the Lehigh Valley, and perhaps through them the Norfolk & Western. He was a friend of Joseph Stalin—a liberal who opposed the confrontational foreign policy of the United States toward the Soviet Union. He was also interested in nuclear arms control and later financed the Pugwash Conference on nuclear arms limitations held in Nova Scotia, where he had been raised. Fortas had successfully defended Eaton against charges of securities violations. Eaton might well have wished to help Fortas.

But for Fortas to communicate through Eaton with my client—even indirectly—without my knowledge and consent constituted unethical conduct. I knew I would win the rate-increase case. Fortas must have held the same view or he would not have violated the canon of ethics. I called Fortas and warned him, "Abe, I do not know whether you have been communicating indirectly with my client through Cyrus Eaton without my knowledge and approval, but if the reverberations don't stop, I'll file a complaint with the ethics committee of the bar association and we'll find out." Tuohy promptly stopped his calls to the Bull Lines officers.

After years of hearings before the Federal Maritime Board and judicial review by the court of appeals, the Bull Lines won the case. By that time American Coal Shipping had discovered that American-flag vessels could not compete with foreign vessels in transporting coal to Europe, a discovery it could have made easily before entering into the business. Lewis's dream was shown to be just that, a dream—like his description of the United States in the remote future. And the A. H. Bull Steamship Company was sold to Manuel Kulukundis, an American ship owner of Greek origin. Fortas went on to other things, including his short-term seat on the Supreme Court.

23

The Black Student Fund

Washington, 1963–1969

AFTER MARION AND I MOVED the family to Washington in 1951, we entered our son, Jonathan, in the Sidwell Friends School, and daughter Katharine a year later. Although Sidwell was a Friends or Quaker school, no American of African descent had ever been enrolled and, as I later learned, there was an admissions policy that children of African ambassadors were the only blacks to be admitted. To its credit, the nearby Florida Avenue Quaker Meeting disassociated itself from the school for this reason.

As in the blues song, at that time Washington was in every respect "a Jim Crow town." Hotels, restaurants, buses, theaters, churches, clubs, and schools were all segregated. Before moving to Washington, while at Paul, Weiss in New York, I had shared a secretary with another associate, Bill Coleman, a black man who had been Justice Felix Frankfurter's law clerk on the Supreme Court. He later assisted Thurgood Marshall in the strategy and execution of the attack on public school segregation that ultimately resulted in *Brown v. Board of Education*. Still later, Coleman served as President Gerald Ford's secretary of transportation. In 1952 or 1953 he called me to say he would be in Washington to file a petition for certiorari and would like to get together. Delighted, I asked Coleman to lunch the next day.

The moment I hung up the phone, I realized the problem: Where? I did not want to ask a friend to lunch only to create an issue concerning the color of my friend's skin. My school and college classmate Adam Yarmolinsky suggested an integrated cafeteria run by the American Veterans Committee. Such was the humble fare to which we were relegated in order to enjoy lunch together in the Nation's Capital! That was one way Washington interpreted our nation's founding claim that all men were created equal.

A childhood friend of Marion's was married in an Episcopal church in Washington. The black lady who had cared for the bride through childhood was relegated to sitting alone in the balcony while the wedding took place below. This is one thing the church meant when it enjoined its parishioners to be Christian.

Shortly after Jonathan entered Sidwell, I began writing letters, often drafted jointly with Marion, to the chairman of Sidwell's board of trustees and the director of the school, urging a change in the admission policy with respect to blacks. I received polite responses stating that the matter was under consideration by the board. Later, when our youngest child, Ellen, was entered in the Potomac School in McLean, Virginia, Marion, and I carefully composed a letter on the same subject to Leonard Meeker, chairman of the Potomac School board and a close friend and neighbor. I never received a written reply to that letter, but the following spring I was elected to the board, which I took to be the answer. From within the board I worked on changing what had been an unexpressed policy of excluding black children from the school. It turned out that there was substantial support for the change among board members and substantial resistance from the school administration.

What often puzzled me was why teachers in independent schools tolerated this exclusionary policy. They were educated people and must have known better. There were a large number of professional blacks in Washington—lawyers, doctors, architects, ministers, teachers in the black public schools, professors at historically black Howard University, business people, and many civil servants. Their children would have added greatly to the life of these schools.

In 1963, Robert Kennedy withdrew his sons from the Landon School in nearby Maryland because the school would not admit black children, and he entered them in an integrated Catholic school. That may have prompted me and Lydia Katzenbach, a good friend, to found the Negro Student Fund. (Lydia was the wife of Nicholas Katzenbach, later attorney general under President Johnson during the civil rights movement.) Our concept was to raise funds to finance tuition for black families who were unable to afford those expenses, so that we could present the schools with qualified black applicants.

Schools would be forced either to accept the child or take specific action to reject a child solely because of the color of his or her skin. Lydia selected Allison MacLean, a member of the Society of Friends, as a founding member of the fund. The others were Walter Ridder, an owner of Ridder Publications; Benjamin Lee Bird, a Washington lawyer; Louis Martin, co-chairman of the Democratic National Committee; and Burma Whitted, a nurse active in educational matters. Louis Martin and Burma Whitted were both black; the others white.

I applied to the IRS to grant the fund charitable status so contributions would be tax deductible. An inordinately long time elapsed while the IRS issued no ruling. We nevertheless raised some funds. At a party at our house on University Terrace in the spring of 1964, I asked Nicholas Katzenbach, who was at that time deputy attorney general, if he thought it appropriate to see whether there were defects in the application to the IRS or whether other considerations were holding up the ruling. Shortly thereafter, the IRS issued a favorable decision. Segregation was deeply embedded in the bureaucracy.

Allison, Burma, and Lydia identified qualified black children to apply to independent schools in the greater Washington area, and a few were admitted in 1963 to a school that was previously open only to whites. (I do not remember which one.) The fund, however, dates its beginning from 1964 when the favorable IRS ruling was issued.

About that time I made an appointment to visit with Paul Landon Banfield, the founder and director of the Landon School, to see whether Attorney General Kennedy's decision to withdraw his sons had had any effect on Landon's admissions policy. It had, but a bad effect. Mr. Banfield came from the South and had a different approach. "I do not regard the Negro as the social equal of the white," he told me. "Times change, however, and I would like one Negro boy in the lower school, one in the middle school, and one in the upper school." It was obvious that he wanted these boys not in order to change policy, but rather to stop discussion. (Throughout the period that I was a trustee of the fund, we took the position that "tokenism" was acceptable as long as it was the beginning of meaningful change.)

It was interesting that Banfield referred only to whether the Negro was the "social" equal of the Caucasian; he did not deprecate the intellectual capacity of blacks. I replied that "under the circumstances, Mr. Banfield, you can find your own Negro boys." Whether the conversation had any subsequent effect on Landon's admissions policy I never learned.

Our interaction with the Sidwell Friends School ended harshly, but differently. Its trustees had long supported a change in admissions policy so that blacks would be admitted on the same basis as whites. Quakers reach decisions on the basis of "a sense of the meeting," a concept not quite the same as consensus but close to it. Sidwell's board chairman, a gentleman of the Old South who had done a great deal for the school in many ways, nevertheless prevented a sense of the meeting on this issue.

I made an appointment with the headmaster, Robert Lyle, for the same purpose as the one with Mr. Banfield at Landon. We discussed the issue for at least two hours. During that period I had asked him to change the existing policy and admit blacks on the same criteria as whites. After all, the admissions office reported to him.

We talked all around this question. At the end he said, "Mr. Schlefer, my contract ends in June, and if I change the policy, my contract will not be renewed." There was no point in continuing the discussion and I excused myself. Just as I was about to reach the door a sudden realization came to me. A sense of the meeting would have to occur among the members of the board before his contract could be renewed. I thought I could ask at least two friends of mine on the board who felt strongly about the issue— Tim Atkinson and Cabot Coville—to prevent a sense of the meeting unless he agreed to end segregation.

I turned and said, "Mr. Lyle, unless you change the policy, I will see to it that your contract is not renewed."

I do not know what happened at the board meeting, and there were probably other issues in play. But Lyle's contract was not renewed. The chairman resigned. The board changed the policy, and Sidwell went forward quickly to integrate. It was not long before 10 percent of the student population was black.

The black students that the fund helped were always children with a strong family structure. It did not matter whether the breadwinner was in one of the professions or behind the wheel of a mail truck. A strong family meant one that was really interested in the children's education.

One striking example was the son of a taxicab driver who was admitted to the Potomac School. The family lived in Anacostia, out of reach of the Potomac School bus. The father drove a taxi at night and returned at two o'clock in the morning for a few hours' sleep. Since his wife did not drive, he drove his son to the Katzenbachs' house in Cleveland Park, where the school bus picked him up. The father went back home, presumably for a few more hours of sleep. In the afternoon he picked up his son, again at the Katzenbach house. The child succeeded at Potomac, not at the top of the class but not at the bottom either.

The Ford Foundation did not support the Negro Student Fund until McGeorge Bundy became its president. In 1968 or 1969, when Lydia Katzenbach and I visited him in New York, he asked us to take on some children of single mothers in deep poverty.

"Mac, it won't work," I warned. "We need a strong family to give support to a child thrust into a white and seemingly alien environment."

"Try ten children," he replied. "I'll make a grant to the fund of $75,000, and all I ask is that you try and—fail or succeed—write a report."

We were able to place nine children in the National Child Research Center in Cleveland Park, near the Katzenbachs' house. It was an excellent preschool (despite the terrible name). The center had a child psychiatrist on staff, held meetings with the mothers of these children two evenings each week, and in other ways made a serious effort to help them succeed. After a few years it became plain that the project was a failure. None of the children was able to handle Potomac, Beauvoir, Sidwell, or other independent schools in the Washington area. The failure was not only caused by lack of support for a child plunged into a school dominated by white children and teachers, but also owing to the lack of a family that could give full daily support for the child's education—a sense at home that education is important in everyone's life. With others on the fund's board, I wrote a detailed report to the Ford Foundation.

The experiment raised a serious question of social policy: How can society create a necessary family structure among single-parent families? How can society motivate children in unconventional households to develop and respect conventional values?

24

Freedom of Information Act:
Mark P. Schlefer v. United States of America

Washington, 1964–1966 et seq.

THE PACIFIC FAR EAST LINE operated several shipping services in transpacific commerce. One of its services was between California and Guam. Some of the Guam vessels went farther, to Indonesia and the Straits Settlements (now Singapore and parts of Malaysia), where they loaded bulk cargo such as raw sugar, rubber, and coconuts ("copra" to the trade). These vessels were slower and had longer turnaround than the vessels that turned at Guam. Around 1963 the company decided that it would also have the slower vessels call at the Marianas, a short diversion from the route to Guam. The company asked me as its counsel in Washington to file a tariff (a schedule of services and charges) with the U.S. Maritime Commission covering the Marianas service, which I did.

In response I received a call from the commission's staff advising me that the tariff was illegal. I asked who had made that determination. The reply was "The general counsel of the commission, Mr. James Pimper."

"May I see a copy of his opinion?"

"We'll ask him."

A day or two later the response came. "Mr. Pimper regards his opinion as confidential."

"Do you really mean his opinion of the applicable law governing the tariff is confidential?"

"Yes."

"Well, in my opinion the tariff complies in all respects with the commission's rules governing tariffs and therefore I am leaving it on file with you. I am advising the Pacific Far East Line that it may operate its Marianas service under the terms of the tariff. If the commission believes the tariff is illegal, it can file a suit in court, but it will have to disclose in court its reason for believing the tariff is illegal."

Shortly thereafter I went to the chairman of the Practice and Procedure Committee of the Administrative Law Section of the American Bar Association and suggested that a bill be drafted to permit access to government documents. Coincidentally, two lawyers on the committee were already starting work on such a bill. "May I join them?" I asked. Other lawyers had had similarly absurd problems with administrative agencies. We drafted what turned out to be the original version of the Freedom of Information Act.

The chairman of the committee took the draft bill to the American Bar Association convention for approval. It won by an overwhelming vote—an enormous help in the legislative process.

Now the task was to get it enacted. I heard that Representative John E. Moss of California had been trying to get documents out of the administration for two years without success. I went to meet the congressman, who took high interest in the idea and asked me to sit down while he read the bill. He read it slowly and carefully, then looked up and said, "Mr. Schlefer, I'll deliver the House. You deliver the Senate." I had no idea how to "deliver" the Senate.

Bernard Fensterwald Jr., a roommate of Ed Ames, one of my close friends at college, was now chief counsel to the Senate Judiciary Committee. I asked Bud if the committee would hold a hearing on the bill. After reading it and talking to the chairman at the time, Senator James Eastland, a conservative Southern Democrat from Mississippi, he agreed.

The *New York Times* and *Washington Post* both declined to support the bill openly, for fear of losing their connections in the federal agencies, although important reporters on each paper wanted them to testify in support. However, the *Wall Street Journal* supported the bill, having suspected corruption in the Small Business Administration office in Richmond, Virginia, and been unable to obtain relevant documents. The three television networks—ABC, NBC, and CBS—all said they would support the legislation if an exception were made for financial information submitted to the government in confidence. Supporters of the bill were not interested in such financial information and agreed to the amendment.

At the hearing, I and the two lawyers who drafted the bill were at the witness table along with several others who had a special interest in the legislation. Representatives of a number of government agencies, which had previously expressed their opposition to the bill, testified in opposition. They were particularly concerned about internal agency memorandums. We were highly interested in the agencies' internal memorandums and would not concede to that exception. Indeed, Mr. Pimper's legal opinion in the Pacific Far East Line matter was an internal memorandum. That was exactly the kind of document that we thought should be made available.

During a recess, I crafted a compromise agreeing to exempt internal agency documents that a court would consider privileged in a litigated case against the agency. This condition satisfied the committee, if not the agencies. In my experience (and in that of others) the exception has never resulted in a court withholding a document under the act.

Of course, the bill excepted some types of documents, such as documents classified for national security reasons, documents related to criminal investigations, or personnel records of employees. As well, the offices of the president and vice president were excluded from the definition of an agency of the United States government so the Freedom of Information Act did not apply to White House documents. Also, the bill did not apply to the District of Columbia government either, though at the time it might have been considered a federal agency. Whether an exception actually applied was to be subject to de novo review by the courts. (De novo review means that the courts could examine as an original matter whether a document was properly within an exception.)

Our revised bill passed both houses of Congress and was sent to the president for his signature. Every member of the president's cabinet recommended a veto. To his everlasting credit, President Lyndon Johnson signed the bill on July 4, 1966. Bud Fensterwald told me that before Johnson signed the bill he said, "I think I may be making a mistake." He signed it anyway.

The Maritime Administration never brought an action to stop the Pacific Far East Line from operating its service to the Marianas.

Those of us who drafted the legislation and worked to obtain its enactment never expected the statute to have the long-term importance that it has achieved. We had a local problem, and we sought to fix it.

In fact, we ended by fixing a crucial national problem. There have been nineteen major U.S. Supreme Court cases under the Freedom of Information Act between 1973 and 2008. There were also important court of appeals decisions that the Supreme Court let stand. For example, Bloomberg News filed a highly significant case in November 2008 to obtain disclosure of the names of the banks that had borrowed from the Federal Reserve's discount window and the amounts borrowed. The U.S. District Court for the Southern District of New York ruled that the Federal Reserve had to disclose the information under the Freedom of Information Act. The court of appeals affirmed and the U.S. Supreme Court refused to review the decision. The amount was $7.77 trillion and the names included many of the largest banks in the world.

An even more recent case having a major impact on the secrecy of the court itself was brought by the Electronic Frontier Foundation in 2011. It sought under the Freedom of Information Act to obtain an 85-page ruling by a judge of the secret Foreign Intelligence Surveillance Court. Judge John D. Bates ordered the release of the opinion, which held that the National Security Agency (NSA) had been violating the U.S. Constitution for several years. The opinion declared that part of the problem was a pattern of misrepresentations by NSA officials in submissions to the secret court.

Every state in the union copied the Freedom of Information Act, as did ninety-three foreign countries. The Freedom of Information Act thus became the principal engine for opening actions of the government to public view.

In 1983 I found that the Maritime Administration was still holding its chief counsel's opinions confidential. I brought an action in the federal courts to settle the matter, asking for all general counsel opinions and the index to them. I lost in the district court, but prevailed on appeal.

Judge Ruth Bader Ginsburg, later a justice on the Supreme Court, wrote the opinion for the district court. Her summary of the case is quoted below (see 226 U.S. App. D.C. 254):

Mark P. SCHLEFER, Appellant,

v.

UNITED STATES of America, et al.

No. 82-1635.

United States Court of Appeals,

District of Columbia Circuit.

Argued January 11, 1983.

Decided March 1, 1983.

As Amended March 1, 1983.

Ruth Bader GINSBURG, Circuit Judge:

The Office of the Chief Counsel of the Maritime Administration maintains summary-indexes of significant written opinions prepared by the Chief Counsel in response to intra-agency requests for legal advice. Many of the indexed "Chief Counsel Opinions" ("ccos") interpret statutes relevant to the Agency's dealings with the public; others address questions of Agency policy, or deal with internal Agency activities. Invoking the Freedom of Information Act (FOIA), 5 U.S.C. Sec. 552, plaintiff-appellant Schlefer seeks release of index digests of ccos that interpret provisions of three statutes assigning prime responsibilities to the Agency: the 1916

Shipping Act, and the 1920 and 1936 Merchant Marine Acts, as amended. The Agency describes these documents as deliberative, predecisional, and within the scope of the attorney-client privilege; it therefore claims that the indexes are shielded by FOIA Exemption 5. In large part, the District Court upheld the Exemption 5 plea. For the reasons set forth below, we hold that the Agency has failed to demonstrate that Exemption 5 covers the CCO summary-indexes in question. Accordingly, we reverse the District Court's judgment and remand the case with instructions to order disclosure of the requested documents.

Years later, on April 26, 2017, Senator Bernie Sanders, the Vermont Democrat, entered the following statement into the *Congressional Record*.

Tribute to MARK SCHLEFER

Mr. SANDERS. Mr. President, I would like to congratulate and honor a Vermont resident for his outstanding commitment to ensuring transparency between the Federal Government and the American public. Mark Schlefer of Putney, VT, played an integral role in the creation of the Freedom of Information Act, FOIA, that came into effect in 1967. Since its incorporation, FOIA has given the American people the right to request to access records from any Federal Agency and has required agencies to post certain categories of information and frequently requested records online.

Mr. Schlefer was inspired to join the legal group that drafted FOIA after working with a shipping client, Pacific Far East Line, which was denied tariff documentation to stop at the Mariana Islands by the Federal Maritime Commission. Mr. Schlefer was upset to find that the Federal Maritime Commission was not required to provide an explanation of the justification behind the rejection.

Along with two other lawyers who came across similar situations with government agencies, Mr. Schlefer helped to draft the legislation for FOIA. After years of working on the bill and convincing both Members of the House and the Senate to support the legislation, it was signed into law by President Lyndon B. Johnson on July 4, 1966.

FOIA helped pave the way for greater government transparency. Increased transparency restores faith in governance by holding government officials accountable to the American people. A truly transparent government roots out systematic waste, fraud and abuse. It is clear that we need to maintain the transparency and accountability of government to the people it is meant to represent. I strongly believe that, as a democracy, we must strive to make our government as transparent as possible and that citizens should be able to obtain information from the government in a reasonable fashion.

Without FOIA, much of the U.S. Government would still be closed off to the American people. This legislation has been an inspiration to other governments and has served as a model throughout the world for opening government information to the public. Since FOIA was enacted nearly 50 years ago, similar Freedom of Information laws have been passed in all 50 States and 93 other nations.

Mark Schlefer has demonstrated an extraordinary level of commitment to ensuring the American people had access to more information throughout the Federal Government. Since its initial enactment, all three branches of the Federal Government have recognized the FOIA as a vital part of our democracy. I heartily applaud Mr. Schlefer for leading the way to a more transparent government, I have no doubt that his outstanding life work has had a significant and positive impact on people and their governments throughout the world.

25

Roosevelt Island New Community

New York City, 1970–1971

I FIRST MET ED LOGUE in 1944 when we both arrived at Syracuse University for pre-cadet simple arithmetic education. We were in a small group that constituted the first class to enter cadet training near San Antonio, Texas. From there we went to different cadet schools and lost contact for the rest of the war. In the next twenty years, our paths crossed fairly frequently.

Ed became president of the New York State Urban Development Corporation. Roosevelt Island—then called Welfare Island—was its flagship project. Adam Yarmolinsky, a close friend of mine both at school in New York and later at Harvard, had come to know Ed at Yale Law School and was appointed president of the Welfare Island Development Corporation. This three-way connection resulted in my appointment in 1970 as general counsel of the Welfare Island corporation. I agreed to spend three days in New York City each week on a pro bono basis. I was paid $200 a day when my law firm charged for my time at $125 an hour. The stipend barely covered the airfare or a room for a night.

The project was to create an entire new town: apartments, a public school for K through 12, a town center with an office building, theater, restaurants, library, playing fields, shops, and parks. It was planned to be mixed income, from subsidized low-income housing ranging upward to market-rate housing. The town was to be free of automobiles except for those associated with the hospital. Small electric buses would transport people on the island. If residents had cars, they were to be parked in a garage on the island-end of the existing bridge over the East River from Queens.

Logue had Gladstone Associates prepare an economic evaluation of the various elements of the plan. Its market-rate housing element seemed on its face overly optimistic. I asked professor Philip David of the Harvard Business School, an expert in real estate, and professor Charles Haar, at the Harvard Law School, a former general counsel of the Department of Housing and Urban Development, to check Gladstone's conclusions. They made a detailed survey of high-income housing in New York and concluded that at the cost levels required, the market-rate housing on the island would not be competitive. I tried to get help from the United Nations, Rockefeller University, and hospitals along the East River. All would have liked to reserve apartments on the island for low-income employees who cleaned the floors, did the laundry, or held similar jobs. I visited officials of several of those institutions and proposed that we agree to reserve apartments for their lower-income employees if they would commit their high-income employees—ambassadors, doctors, professors—to live in market-rate housing, which we would then build. They declined, so we declined. As a result of the careful study that Haar and David had made, the market-rate housing was deferred.

Normal access to and from the island was to be via a funicular suspended on a track running from East 59th Street along the underside of the Queensboro Bridge. I tried to persuade Bloomingdale's to pay part of the cost of the funicular in return for putting the station inside the store. But the management declined the opportunity. So we declined. A Swiss ski-lift company designed and built the funicular.

One of the most frustrating (and amusing) parts of getting the construction under way was the ordeal of obtaining the dozens of city permits that were required. It took only about three weeks to get a permit from the U.S. Army Corps of Engineers in Washington, required because the construction would be over a navigable waterway, the East River. Weeks of pounding the halls of New York City government offices failed to obtain the many needed city permits. I went to see Mayor John Lindsay, who assigned one of his bright young assistants to help me. She and I again made the rounds of the city departments, but still to no avail.

The New York State Urban Development Corporation had legal authority to set aside local ordinances, a power it rarely used. If the project was ever to go forward, that power had to be used now. The Welfare Island board of directors included the heads of many of the relevant city offices, including the mayor, the borough presidents of Queens and Manhattan, the president of the city council, and the parks commissioner. I made a presentation, and after some discussion the board voted to set aside the ordinances that required the permits. Even that failed to solve the problem because police officers on site had to see permits before they would let work start, and we did not have permits. I asked one of the architects to design permits with the seal of the corporation, a facsimile signature, and the like. That expedient seemed to satisfy the police, and construction finally got under way.

A number of the major contractors and developers in New York came to talk to me about bidding on constructing the apartments and the office building. The most striking was a developer who wanted a contract to erect all the structures on the island. He would then build a factory upstate on the Hudson River to manufacture prefabricated segments of the buildings, float them on barges down the Hudson to the East River, and assemble the buildings on the island.

Because the building trade unions had been blocking industrialized housing for years, I asked, "What would you do about the union rules?"

"Well," he replied, "I would apply the Golden Rule."

"What do you mean, the Golden Rule?"

"He who has the gold makes the rules."

It was never clear how he was going to use his gold. Would he just pay much higher wages for the work he needed, or would he try to bribe union leaders? Just at this time (1970) the Port Authority of New York was building the World Trade Center towers (destroyed on September 11, 2001). That construction was employing 40 percent of all the electricians in the greater New York area and probably a similar percentage of the other building trades. If the project was going to be built, a fight with building trades was out of the question.

We put each structure on Roosevelt Island up for competitive bid separately on a fixed-price basis. This procedure served to protect the project when roaring inflation began to rise soon thereafter.

The most interesting and imaginative part of the project was the school, which was designed to implement two principles. The first was that small schools are as important as small classes, because they enable each child to be a known person, and to know the others in the community. The second principle was that low-income adults and children behave better when they are in each other's company.

The very architecture of the schools helped implement these principles. The schools were built into the lower floors of the apartment buildings and limited to no more than two hundred students each. There were no dining halls. The students were given vouchers, which they could use at town restaurants. There was no school library; students were to use the town library. The town's playing fields were the schools' playing fields. The town theater was the schools' theater.

One task was to get this plan approved by the New York City Board of Education. As with the permits for constructing the funicular, it was hard to change settled ways that demanded large schools, thick walls, dark halls, a library, dining rooms, and similar prison-like features. Fortunately, a thoughtful, imaginative superintendent of schools, an African American, had been brought to New York City from New England. He fully appreciated the ideas behind the Welfare Island plan. He and I visited individual members of the board to discuss the ideas for the schools. Approval was finally won.

Jose Luis Sert, a prominent architect originally from Catalonia who designed important buildings in Spain, France, and the United States, had won the American Institute of Architecture's gold medal and became dean of the Harvard Graduate School of Design. He was selected for many of the buildings on the island. Sert made his own creative suggestions. For example, he thought that old people liked to be with children, and young children generally liked old people. He thus proposed locating housing for the elderly adjacent to the lower school, so that children and the elderly could meet in the garden. As elderly people often also would like quiet and some distance from children, Sert additionally designed a quiet garden on the other side of the house for the elderly, away from the children.

I served as general counsel until 1971, by which time most of the construction contracts were in place. Then I could return to my fulltime practice in Washington, and to my family.

26

The Bucharest City Plan and Citizen Participation

Romania, 1972

LEONARD MEEKER HAD BEEN a close friend since our earliest days in Washington. His first wife, Christine, had been a very special friend of Marion's until her early death at thirty-five. Their children and ours had also been friends.

Leonard was deputy legal adviser to the State Department during the Kennedy administration and he became legal advisor during the Johnson years. As Secretary of State Dean Rusk once observed, Leonard was the conscience of the department. After Richard Nixon was elected president in 1968, Leonard was appointed ambassador to Romania.

In 1972, Leonard and his second wife, Beverly, invited Marion and me to visit Bucharest and stay with them in the ambassador's residence. We accepted with pleasure and stopped en route to Athens. Bucharest was remarkable for the absence of suburban sprawl; the city was transformed to a country landscape at the margin. Driving into the countryside, we found ourselves quite lost on rural roads used by hay wagons without lights and we were almost late to dinner.

Leonard had invited people he thought would interest us. There was the Greek ambassador, the editor of a weekly news magazine similar to *Time*, the husband of a ballet dancer who was traveling abroad with a dance company, and perhaps also the British ambassador. One of the conversations, particularly with the editor, related to censorship, which no one feared discussing—at least in the embassy.

Leonard also organized for the next morning a small gathering of Romanian officials concerned with the Bucharest city plan. He arranged for them to meet with us because Marion had for some years been an urban analyst in the Legislative Reference Service (later the Congressional Research Service), and I had been counsel to the development corporation that built the new town on Roosevelt Island.

At the gathering, in addition to a translator, were the city architect, the city engineer, the city planner, as well as Beverly with her infant daughter, Leonard, Marion, and me. The table was rather long, with the Romanians on one side and the Americans on the other. A large map of Bucharest was affixed to the wall behind the Romanians. Beverly was nursing her baby, Eliza, startling the strait-laced Romanians.

All present were served coffee and, at about eleven o'clock, a wineglass of what I took to be sherry. It turned out to be a strong Romanian brandy called Tuica. I started to reach for the coffee when Marion whispered, "You must wait for the ambassador to lift his cup first." Time went by. The ambassador failed to lift his cup. I thought that my good friend would not be offended, and reached for my cup. Immediately everyone around the table reached for his or her cup. As Leonard later explained, Marion and I were the "honored" guests and the others had been waiting for us to begin.

The three Romanian professionals proceeded to explain, through the interpreter, the plans for Bucharest. The Americans freely asked questions about parts of the plan. Then Marion asked, "Do you have citizen participation?"

"Oh, yes," was the reply. "There is a model of the plan in the main public library with a stack of postcards, already stamped, for the purpose of permitting the citizens to offer their comments and mail them to the appropriate office. The comments of people that like the plan and agree with us, we keep, and those that do not we discard."

That was more citizen participation than occurred at Roosevelt Island, which treated its board of directors as the "citizens" for purposes of "citizen participation." The board had included the mayor, the Queens and Manhattan borough presidents, the parks commissioner, the curator of the Metropolitan Museum of Art, and similar representatives of the New York City establishment. On neither side of the Iron Curtain did we want the citizens to mess up the plan.

From Romania we went to Athens, where at five thirty in the morning we visited the Acropolis. The early morning light was extraordinarily beautiful as the sun slanted over the classical buildings and sculptures on the most famous hill in the Western world. We enjoyed it alone; no busloads of tourists had yet arrived for the day.

27

Playing God

Washington, 1980s

BARBARA TOVEY WAS A classmate and close friend of Marion's at Swarthmore College. For many years Barbara's husband, George Tovey, taught philosophy at Mount Holyoke College, and she taught English at Smith College. Their son, Peter, was a man of high intelligence. He earned a doctorate at MIT without ever having obtained a bachelor's degree, and became an assistant professor at Brown University on a tenure track.

It is possible, even probable, that drugs got the better of Peter and turned his life into a sad and lonely one. He became anti-black, contrary to all the traditions of his upbringing. He wandered to Washington, D.C., thence to Florida. He was jailed in Tampa for some minor infraction of the law, but had to be separated from other prisoners because giving voice to his bigotry might have incited them to harm him. His parents had been professionally advised not to support him. He was nevertheless able to return to Washington, where he stayed with a former student.

Peter was now in his early or mid-forties. He had drafted a letter containing the following threat, as I remember it: "[President George H. W.] Bush must be killed. [Vice President Dan] Quayle must be killed. [signed] Peter Tovey." The former student became concerned and advised the Secret Service about the letter, though it was never mailed. Peter was arrested. Barbara and George called and asked me to represent Peter at the arraignment. I talked with him beforehand and persuaded him to consent to a guardianship, believing that the court would appoint his mother as guardian.

At the hearing before a magistrate of the U.S. District Court for the District of Columbia, Peter changed his mind and refused to agree to a guardianship. The magistrate was persuaded to commit him to St. Elizabeth's Hospital for a psychiatric examination. He was diagnosed as a severe manic-depressive. I could not effectively communicate with Peter or obtain guidance concerning his objectives.

A meeting was scheduled in the chambers of Judge Joyce Hens Green. Her father had been a psychiatrist, and she proved sympathetic. The Secret Service, as represented by the U.S. attorney's office, was not particularly concerned about Peter creating a serious danger to either the president or vice president, but the service wanted him out of Washington. If the case had gone to trial on the basis of a complaint or a grand jury indictment, I very possibly could have won on the grounds that the threatening letter had not been mailed, no act had occurred, the U.S. Postal Service had not been used, and literally nothing had happened. That would have released Peter to wander the streets, a danger to himself and to others.

Judge Green believed that only the state court in the state of his residence could appoint a guardian without Peter's consent. In the absence of any ability to engage in a rational discussion with him or a legally constituted guardian, I had only the authority the court informally recognized. It was agreed that Peter would be sent to a federal mental hospital in Rochester, Minnesota, for treatment.

After six months or so, Judge Green called me and advised that she could no longer hold Peter without a trial. In fact, the American Civil Liberties Union in Minnesota was about to ask a federal court there to order Peter's release. Having supported the ACLU all of my life, I was sympathetic to this view, but as a practical matter to release Peter would have been dangerous.

Making all these judgments and decisions without the guidance based on the normal lawyer-client relationship made me feel as if I were playing God.

At my suggestion, Peter's mother, Barbara, then living in Hanover, New Hampshire, after George's death, was able to prevail upon a New Hampshire state hospital to accept Peter as a patient. Judge Green agreed to the transfer. A state court, with the aid of a lawyer in New Hampshire representing

Barbara, appointed her as Peter's guardian. Barbara subsequently arranged to have him transferred to a hospital in Massachusetts; he died at the age of seventy-three.

28

An Amazing Woman

Washington, 1981–1982

MARION WAS ELECTED chair of the Committee of 100 on the Federal City, an organization composed of architects and planners in and around Washington, D.C. as well as others interested or involved in planning and architecture.

In about 1981, Dr. Arthur M. Sackler, a medical entrepreneur and philanthropist, donated his collection of Asian art to the Smithsonian Institution along with some cash for a building to house the collection and other Asian art.

Marion objected to the location proposed by the Smithsonian and persuaded the Committee of 100 to support her suggestion for another site. When the Smithsonian rejected her suggestion, she asked for a hearing before the planning commission. The Smithsonian is one of the most powerful institutions in Washington. It has important senators and members of Congress on its board and always has close connections with whatever administration is in power in Washington.

The Smithsonian sent six witnesses to testify before the planning commission (though I remember only one of them, Muriel Humphrey, widow of Vice President Hubert

Humphrey). Marion alone testified for the Committee of 100. When she came home that evening she said to me, "There I was, a little old lady in slippers, and I prevailed over the Smithsonian Institution."

I replied, "You were not little, you were not old, and you were not in slippers, but you were a lady, every inch a lady, and you dealt with the merits, not who you are."

In due course the Arthur M. Sackler Gallery was built at its present site—which Marion had proposed beside the Smithsonian "Castle" on the National Mall.

29

Philippine Labor, Muslims and Whisky!

Washington and Kuwait, 1984

DURING THE REAGAN YEARS there was a brutal war between Iraq and Iran involving poison gas in the Persian Gulf region. The Kuwaiti government wanted to place its tankers under the U.S. flag to obtain the protection of the U.S. Navy, and they retained me to re-flag their vessels accordingly. In connection with the re-flagging, I gave the Kuwait Oil Company an opinion that it could retain the Philippine crews serving on its vessels as long as the vessels did not call at American ports. This was because the statute provided that an American-flag vessel must have a U.S.–citizen crew only "upon each departure from the United States."

The American seafaring unions were furious. They persuaded the House Merchant Marine and Fisheries Committee to hold a hearing. It was the strangest of hearings. I couldn't understand the chairman, Walter Jones, a North Carolinian, and he couldn't understand me. The chief counsel interpreted each of us for the other. I told the Committee, "I only interpret the law. You gentlemen make the law. If you don't like it, change it." They did exactly that, but it took a year and half or two years to do it. After that, I obtained a waiver from the Defense Department for two years.

Meanwhile, the unions brought a lawsuit against the Kuwait Oil Company to force it to pay its crews the minimum wage established by the Fair Labor Standards Act of 1938. I was retained by the company, and to prepare the case I went to Kuwait, where I had a couple of memorable experiences.

In Kuwait I wanted to see the interior of the large mosque, but since Marion and I had not been permitted to go into a mosque in Egypt (because we were not Muslims), I inquired at the door. I was told that as long as I took off my shoes I could enter. "Muhammad welcomed all to the mosque," the attendant remarked. I appreciated the civility expressed then on behalf of the Prophet, and I appreciate it even more today.

One evening I was invited to a grand house on the Persian Gulf (called "the Arabian Gulf" locally) for a special dinner. I was seated next to the oil minister, who asked what I'd like to drink. Having in mind that Muslims don't drink alcoholic beverages, I asked for Perrier with a bit of lime. The oil minister ordered a water glass half full of Scotch with ice.

30

Nuclear Bombs

Washington, 1996

AFTER AUGUST 6, 1945, thoughtful members of my generation lived in the shadow of a thermonuclear exchange. Albert Einstein remarked, "Everything has changed except the way we think." At about the same time, J. Robert Oppenheimer expressed deep concern about the likely proliferation of nuclear arms.

"They are not too hard to make," Oppenheimer told colleagues in the Manhattan Project, which designed and built the atomic bombs that we used to end World War II. "They will be universal if people wish to make them universal." And in 1963 President Kennedy predicted that in fifteen or twenty years as many as twenty-five nations might have nuclear weapons.

At the height of the nuclear arms race, the five nuclear-weapons states—the United States, the United Kingdom, France, the Soviet Union, and Red China—together held about seventy thousand bombs. By far the greatest numbers were in arsenals of the United States and the Soviet Union.

Modern strategic nuclear weapons typically have from twelve to fifteen times the explosive power of the Hiroshima bomb. Since one properly placed bomb could immolate any major city, the race to a total of seventy thousand was collective insanity.

In 1994 I was elected president of the Lawyers Alliance for World Security. LAWS, a nationwide arms control organization founded by lawyers, has a substantial number of other professionals on its board, including former government officials and experts in all aspects of arms control. The board included such distinguished figures as Bob McNamara, Bill Colby and Stansfield Turner.[1]

---

[1] Here is a more complete roster of board members and the senior positions they had held: Robert McNamara, secretary of defense; Stanley Resor, under secretary of defense; Adam Yarmolinsky, special assistant to McNamara, counsel to the Arms Control and Disarmament Agency (ACDA), and chairman of LAWS; Paul Warnke, director of ACDA and assistant secretary of defense for national security affairs; Ralph Earl, another director of ACDA and chairman of LAWS; William Colby, director of the CIA; Admiral Stansfield Turner, also director of the CIA; John Holum, director of ACDA; George Bunn, counsel to the group that negotiated the NPT; John Rhinelander, counsel to the negotiators of SALT 1; Larry Korb, assistant secretary of defense; Elizabeth Rindskopf, general counsel to the CIA; Louis B. Sohn, Harvard Law School professor; David Koplow, Georgetown School of Law professor; Stephen Dycus, Vermont Law School professor; Bruce Blair, founder of the National Security Institute and executive producer of the film *Countdown to Zero;* James Goodby, vice chairman of the U.S. delegation to the Strategic Arms Reduction Talks (START); and Phil Fleming, Louise Walker Resor, Hans Loeser, Nancy Ignatius, Susan Eisenhower, Ellen Craig, Palmer Smith, Seth Grae, Joe Cirincione, and Tony Sager. Erwin Griswold, dean of Harvard Law School and solicitor general of the United States, served as honorary chairman.

This was not a letterhead board. The members regularly attended meetings, held by telephone conference approximately monthly, and actively helped form and implement policies and programs. After I persuaded Tom Graham, former general counsel of the U.S. Arms Control and Disarmament Agency, to be president of LAWS in 1997, I became vice chairman and subsequently chairman.

LAWS was active in all forms of arms control. It had a significant impact on the 1993 Chemical Weapons Convention and the 1996 Comprehensive Nuclear-Test-Ban Treaty, which has been signed but not yet ratified. However, once the treaty had been signed, the United States became legally bound not to take any action contrary to the purpose of the treaty. Hence the United States has ceased testing since the treaty was signed. LAWS tried in many meetings with government officials in major European countries to obtain a "no first use" agreement by all governments having a nuclear weapon. It was frustrated in this effort not by China, Russia, or Europe, but by American policy. The United States would not even permit the subject to be put on the NATO agenda.

LAWS also worked with foreign governments, particularly the Russian Federation, China, and several of the former Soviet republics, on regulations to limit the export of nuclear technology and materials. In the spring of 1995 LAWS worked hard to help obtain indefinite extension of the 1968 Nuclear Non-Proliferation Treaty (NPT), which had been due to expire. The NPT had become effective in 1970. With the exception of Israel's arsenal, and one or two bombs developed by South Africa and later destroyed after apartheid was abolished, the NPT was, for about twenty-five years, able to limit nuclear-weapon capability to the five permanent members of the United Nations Security Council. Those five were permitted by the NPT to have nuclear weapons temporarily. But about 1995, coincident with its indefinite extension, the treaty began to fall apart and proliferation began to spread.

The spread of nuclear weapons occurs out of fear, military rivalry, or desire to achieve prestige and status. It is possible that in 1946 possession of a nuclear weapon by the United States deterred the Red Army, after it had taken over most of Eastern Europe, from marching across Germany and France to the North Sea. That, and other obvious reasons, motivated the Soviet Union to do everything in its power, including espionage, to obtain the bomb.

The longest, most heavily armed frontier in the world is between Russia and China. Once the Soviets had the bomb, China had to develop the technology to build a bomb. China, in turn, fought four armed conflicts with India in the postwar period. This, presumably, is what drove India to build a bomb. Pakistan, always in conflict with India, came next. Israel, in 1956, helped France and England in their military effort to retake the Suez Canal, a conflict that the United States stopped in its tracks. After that event, fearing that it could not always depend upon the United States, and being in a constant state of war with its Arab neighbors, Israel decided to build a nuclear arsenal, always pretending that it had no bomb. But it never signed the NPT, a strong indication with other evidence that it had the bomb. With the exception of Arab countries, particularly Egypt, the world seemed to tolerate Israel's arsenal, perhaps on the theory that as long as it was the superpower of the Middle East with conventional weapons there was little fear that it would use the bomb.

During the 1980s Iran had a savage eight-year war with Iraq, which used poison gas against it and was then trying to develop nuclear weapons. The United States after 1979 also became a threat to Iran. It responded by starting a nuclear-weapons program of its own, claiming it was only seeking peaceful uses of nuclear energy—hardly believable since Iran was sitting on the second-largest oil reserves and per-haps the largest gas reserves in the Middle East. In developing nuclear weapons, Iran, a Shiite nation, may also have feared the nuclear weapons of its Sunni neighbor, Pakistan. Israel's widely assumed possession of the bomb probably also motivated both Iraq and Iran to seek nuclear-weapons capability.

North Korea had, in the absence of a peace treaty, been in a legal state of war with the United Nations, represented primarily by the United States, which was doing all in its power to isolate that country from the world. North Korea believed it needed the bomb and a missile capability to threaten American territory.

Where next? Saudi Arabia, sitting on huge oil and gas reserves, is planning to build capacity for peaceful uses of atomic energy, which can quickly lead to the building of a nuclear weapon. Will one or more of the former Soviet republics seek a bomb to protect themselves from Russia?

The nuclear bomb is becoming the weapon of the weak, and the strong are frustrated in efforts to stop proliferation. Given the human propensity toward war, is there any hope for breaking this fearful slide toward the destruction of civilization? One possibility is a multilateral treaty eliminating all nuclear weapons. This in truth is called for by Article VI of the NPT. It calls on all parties "to pursue negotiations in good faith on effective measures relating to cessation of the nuclear arms race at an early date and to nuclear disarmament, and on a treaty of general and complete disarmament under strict and effective international control."

Article VI thus sets forth obligations to negotiate in good faith toward three independent objectives: (1) an early cessation of the nuclear arms race by the United States and Russia, which has been accomplished; (2) nuclear disarmament; and (3) a treaty of general and complete disarmament.

In a unanimous 1996 advisory decision, the International Court of Justice said that Article VI requires all signatories to achieve "nuclear disarmament in all its aspects" by "pursuing negotiations on the matter in good faith" (Legality of the Threat or Use of Nuclear Weapons, 1996. I.C.J. Report 226, Advisory Opinion of July 8, 1996).

The barrier to achieving this legal obligation is that there is no effective way of enforcing such a treaty. The normal method of enforcing a treaty against noncompliance by some parties is to relieve parties that are in compliance of their obligation to comply. It would be a disaster if all parties were relieved of their obligations under a nuclear disarmament treaty because one party violated the treaty.

After a dozen years of working on arms control with some of the most knowledgeable people on the subject, my conclusion is that we need a treaty along the following lines: It would gradually effect a reduction in the number of weapons possessed by nuclear powers to, say, three or four hundred. The treaty should also provide that the warheads be disassembled, separated from delivery vehicles, and maintained at a distance that would require two or three days to reassemble. All these measures would be subject to detailed on-site inspection at any time, anywhere, without advance notice. There should be provisions for publicizing violations and providing for applying progressively stricter sanctions. In addition, the treaty should require individual nations to cease production of enriched uranium, plutonium, or any material that could fuel a fission bomb. A central internationally supervised facility would produce fissile material for peaceful uses of nuclear power, and its use would be subject to the verification procedure. Finally, a comprehensive test ban should be a part of the treaty.

As long as the major powers complied with such a treaty it would be enforceable, and if one major power committed a breach, the others could reassemble their warheads and delivery vehicles. The immense deterrent of even a single modern strategic nuclear warhead would powerfully persuade compliance with such a treaty.

31

Murder II

Washington, circa 2009

DURING THE COURSE of my law practice in Washington I made three friends on the Court of Appeals for the D.C. Circuit: David Bazelon, the chief judge of that court for many years and a neighbor on University Terrace; Harold Leventhal, whom I came to know when he was chief counsel for the Office of Price Stabilization during the Korean War; and Carl McGowan, who had been in Governor Adlai Stevenson's administration in Springfield, Illinois. The price of my friendships was to be frequently appointed to serve without compensation as counsel in criminal cases to indigent defendants. It was possibly a measure of the court's confidence in me and my firm. But the firm and I spent much time reading the records of lower court cases, developing defenses, sometimes interviewing defendants, and arguing these cases before the court of appeals.

I was once appointed to defend a man who had been convicted in the trial court of first-degree murder and sentenced to die. This defendant, like the others I had represented, was a part of the sub-culture in Washington,

D.C. Unlike the other court-appointed cases, this one unnerved me. The man's very life depended on my competence as counsel in a kind of case for which I had no special expertise, no large experience, and no other particular qualification. Somehow a capital case made other criminal cases seem trivial.

The homicide had occurred on upper 14th Street Northwest. The defendant had sold heroin to the victim, was trying to collect the payment, and in the course of that effort shot and killed the victim. The only eyewitness to testify in the trial court was an eight-year-old boy who said the defendant was not the man who killed the victim. Other evidence pointed almost definitively to the defendant as the killer, and the jury convicted him of first-degree murder. The trial judge sentenced him to death.

I saw two possible issues on appeal. The more interesting was the fact that the trial judge had excluded from the jury every potential juror who had a conscientious objection to the death penalty. Was it a constitutional jury? The other was the judge's failure to define for the jury the meaning of "beyond a reasonable doubt." I discussed these two issues fully in my brief on appeal. The Supreme Court had not then decided the constitutional issue.

At the oral argument Harold Leventhal presided over the three-judge panel. Being counsel for the appellant, I would normally open and close the arguments. No sooner had I arisen to present my argument when Judge Leventhal said, "Never mind, Mr. Schlefer. The court wants to hear what the government has to say." The judges questioned the government counsel closely on both issues I had raised in my brief. When I rose to respond to the government's arguments, Judge Leventhal said, "Never mind, Mr. Schlefer. Case submitted."

About three weeks later a decision came down. It did not mention the constitutional issue, but discussed only the trial judge's erroneous charge regarding reasonable doubt, and on that ground reversed his judgment. On remand I was able to persuade the government to reduce the charge to second-degree manslaughter, which substituted a jail sentence for the death penalty.

Years later the Supreme Court held that excusing every potential juror who had a conscientious objection to the death penalty did not cause a constitutional defect in the composition of the jury. I am of the view that the Supreme Court was wrong. The other jurors voting to convict might yet persuade the juror with a conscientious objection to the death penalty that death is what the law contemplates as a possibility and they are sworn to uphold the law. The objecting juror might be persuaded that sentencing is for the judge, or, as it is now, for a separate sentencing jury, and does not offend his conscience. The other jurors, on the other hand, might be persuaded by the objecting juror to convict on a lesser charge. All of these possibilities are reasonable results and do not warrant excusing all potential jurors who have a conscientious objection to the death penalty. The constitutional jury should reflect the ethical standards of the community, which includes those members who, on moral grounds, do not believe in capital punishment.

I had two other brushes with capital punishment, worth a postscript to this incident. Some years later the Council of the District of Columbia called for a referendum on whether the death penalty should be abolished. I worked with other lawyers to get capital punishment abolished. It was in fact abolished, although not owing to our efforts. It was the community of black ministers inveighing against the death penalty, Sunday after Sunday, that carried the day.

Still later, in 2009, the American Law Institute considered the matter of the death penalty in drafting its Model Penal Code. The institute's council, its governing body, recommended that no position be taken on the issue and that the former provision establishing restrictive conditions for administering the death penalty simply be deleted. This treatment, in my view, had the effect of tolerating the death penalty. The membership, after three hours of debate, voted for elimination of the capital punishment provision "in light of the current intractable institutional and structural obstacles to ensuring a minimally adequate system for administering capital punishment." Implicitly it declined to state that for this reason capital punishment should no longer be a penal option.

It seemed to me that if the criminal justice system could not ensure "a minimally adequate system for administering capital punishment" it should not be a penal option. I sent the following letter to Roberta Cooper Ramo, president of the ALI, and received the next one in response:

Dear Ms. Ramo:

If you think it would be appropriate, would you bring my thoughts, outlined herein, to the attention of the Council when it considers the capital punishment question?

While I voted for the compromise amendment to Mr. Leahy's motion to amend, on reflection I think that was a mistake and the Council in my view should not endorse the action of the members. That action in addition to withdrawing section 210.6 from the Model Penal Code proclaimed that it was doing so: "...in light of the current intractable institutional and structural obstacles to en-suring a minimally adequate system for administering capital punishment." If that became the Institute's position, how could it remain indifferent as to whether capital punishment continues to be a penal option?

There were two significant reasons for declining to take a position against capital punishment: first, that because of deep personal convictions with respect to capital punishment, "careful study and reasoned debate... would probably not contribute to the political debate on capital punishment or influence the views of legal policymakers" (paragraph 5 of the Council's Report to the Membership); and second, that the Institute had not made its own study of the issue.

The first is not borne out by the evidence. A bipartisan study in Illinois resulted in an indefinite moratorium on the death penalty and a similar study in New Jersey persuaded the legislature to abolish the death penalty. In Maryland a study of the effect on the victim's family of long, drawn-out death-penalty proceedings, among other parts of the study, resulted in an indefinite moratorium on capital punishment. The Steiker Report lists a number of other studies by states having the death penalty (Annex B to the Council's Report to the Membership, pages 3–4).

Careful study and reasoned debate in truth do influence policymakers to take action.

With respect to the second point, as I understand from Annexes 6 and 7, the Program Committee recommended that a study of the death penalty be made, and the Council, subject to certain qualifications and understandings, agreed, and authorized the Director to appoint qualified persons to make the study. The President and the Executive Committee were to consult about presenting the matter to the membership. The Steikers were engaged and presented their Report to an ALI-sponsored conference, as a result of which certain changes were made in the Report with the consent of the Steikers.

The Report to the Membership, in addition, stated, "The [Steiker] paper is very much what the ALI leadership had wanted and has helped the Program Committee and the Council's deliberations enormously." All of this gave the Council and the leadership of the Institute a certain responsibility for the Steiker Report.

The Report was then submitted to the membership "for information and not for approval" (Footnote 2, page 3, of the Council's Report to the Membership). Nevertheless, the membership, after almost three hours of discussion, by a voice vote in fact approved the conclusion of the Steiker Report, quoted above, except for the recommendation that the death penalty should not be a penal option.

If the Institute cannot take a position condemning the death penalty as a penal option without making its own study, how could it recommend withdrawing section 210.6 from the Model Penal Code without such a study? The answer must be that under the circumstances of this special issue the Steiker Report, at this stage at least, is an ALI study and permits action on both section 210.6 and condemnation of the death penalty.

This is not a large segment of the law, which calls for reporters, advisors, views of the Council and the members over many years. It relates to one section of the Model Penal Code. The Council should in my view add condemnation of capital punishment to the action of the members, and so recommend to the membership next year.

To put the discussion in a lighter vein may I suggest the members of the Council read or reread *Measure for Measure*? The death penalty drives the drama from beginning to end. The judge, Angelo, is a principal character and is given one of the great soliloquies in the corpus of Shakespeare's plays, a soliloquy of self-discovery and self-evaluation.

And Isabella's plea for mercy for her condemned brother is at least the equal of Portia's in *The Merchant of Venice*. While the end is somewhat forced, nobody's head goes to the chopping block, not even the judge's, who claims he deserves it, because he committed the same crime for which he sentenced Claudio. The play probably is the mature Shakespeare's reflection on the workings of legal justice on human frailty. The title of the play must be Shakespeare's judgment of what law is all about.

I thought I would send a copy of this letter to three members of the Council, Roswell Perkins, Hugh Calkins and Louis Pollak, who long ago shared with me our student days.

Sincerely,

Mark P. Schlefer

The letter I received in response read:

Dear Mark:

Thank you for your enormously thoughtful letter concerning our deliberations and the possibility of future action by the ALI Council on issues relating to capital punishment and withdrawing Section 210.6 of the Model Penal Code.

I will, of course, share your thoughts both with the Program Committee and our entire Council. While as you point out the debate was fulsome, our bicameral governance and the conflicts between the Council's recommendation and the Membership's action are worth serious consideration. I appreciate your setting out so elegantly your view of what the substance of the discussion and action was and your suggested action for the Council.

We will of course also share with you the result of Council deliberations, which may take both the October and December meeting to come to conclusion.

What an extraordinary group of students you four must have been. We are all lucky to have the benefit of your current wisdom. Of course in this case I hope that all's well that ends well.

/signed/

Roberta Cooper Ramo

Sixty years earlier, Sheldon Glueck, a professor at Harvard Law School, and his wife, Eleanor, after studying all aspects of the death penalty, came to the conclusion that there was no moral or practical justification for the death penalty. As one of his students, I could not have thought that sixty years later I would still be struggling with that issue.

32

Teaching Ethics

Putney, Vermont, 2012

WE HAVE A CRISIS IN ETHICS in this country. I proposed a partial solution to the Putney town school board when I was a member. Here are some examples of the crisis in ethics:

- President George W. Bush and Vice President Dick Cheney pushed us into a war in Iraq on the representation that nuclear arms or other weapons of mass destruction were in Iraq President Saddam Hussein's hands. There were no such arms and they had never had evidence of such. Thousands of young Americans and young citizens of other NATO countries thus died in a false cause.

- More recently, officers of Enron Corporation cooked the books, and touted its stock to the public while they were selling their own stock, knowing that the corporation was failing. Similarly, the princes and barons of Wall Street made mortgage loans to indigent people who could never have afforded to pay back the interest and principal. These so-called subprime mortgages were packaged and the packages sold to others under high and unwarranted credit ratings. Still further, almost every week on the business pages of the *New York Times* some corporations are being fined and some officers being tried for white-collar crimes.

• The CIA, which probably has more staff with PhD degrees than the rest of the government put together, was guilty of widespread torture and also of rendition to countries they knew practiced torture.

• Six Volkswagen executives were charged with criminal misdoing as that company pled guilty in its emissions case.

• Wells Fargo managers fueled the creation of bogus accounts.

• The U.S. Chamber of Commerce is lobbying to get the Foreign Corrupt Practices Act of 1977 repealed so that U.S. companies can bribe foreign government officials without violating American law. Never mind that bribery is wrong.

We tend to think that corruption is pervasive only in less developed countries. Not so.

David Brooks of the *New York Times* called attention to a study by Christian Smith and a distinguished group of sociologists of the moral judgments of young Americans from across the United States with appalling revelations.

About the only wrongs they agreed on were that murder and rape were bad. These young people uniformly thought conduct was moral as long as they "felt good about it."

While I don't think we can do away with evil in the world by teaching ethics in school, I do believe that we can awaken people's awareness of ethical values. I believe that if children were taught to look at their other studies and the events in the world at large from an ethical-value perspective, we could substantially reduce the fraud and twisted values that now pervade our society. As you will see, there are large chunks of education in the classes I propose.

Ethics is really not a course. It is more like an introduction to moral issues. It would be only one class period a week in all grades. There would be no homework, no tests, and no defined subject matter. There would be questions, discussions, and perhaps arguments. The teacher would not really be a teacher but rather a convener, a questioner, and a storyteller. In most cases there would be no correct answer, as different cultures have different standards, and any one culture may contain different and conflicting values. One half-time additional teacher could teach all grades, since it would, in each grade, be only one period a week.

How would it work? What would happen in class? The storyteller would first tell one or two stories and then ask questions about them. In one story, the storyteller might ask about the values in the culture at the time of the story and compare them with our values. And if there were two stories, the values in each could be compared. Students may be asked to take different sides of an issue, with each side defending its view of the issue. The idea is for the storyteller to generate discussion among the students about ethical standards. The discussion based on one story or two companion stories might last over some weeks. The procedure should, as a further by-product, allow students to practice supporting their positions orally.

Our storyteller is not expected to read to, or read with, our students, but he or she should know and love the stories, be able occasionally to read passages from them, and help students think about the moral issues. One of the purposes of the suggested ethics course is to familiarize our students with the great stories of the past, such as the Greek myths. They may then want to return to the original works later in life.

Let me give you some examples, starting with the Declaration of Independence or perhaps such novels as Victor Hugo's *Les Misérables* (though I do not expect first graders to read such works). My ethics teacher can tell the relevant portion of a story, and the pupils can then discuss the rights and wrongs of the actions in the story. In addition to making value judgments, I want my young scholars to think critically. At the end of this chapter I will describe some living situations to expose older children to actual issues in the community.

To begin, then, let us turn to that great proclamation, the Declaration of Independence. What was going on in Thomas Jefferson's mind when he penned the words "all men are created equal, that they are endowed by their Creator with certain inalienable Rights, that among these are Life, Liberty and the pursuit of Happiness?" He himself held human beings bound in slavery and is known to have stood by while his foreman lashed a slave for a minor infraction. He mortgaged slaves as property to pay for his way of life. When he died his slaves were sold to pay his debts. That Declaration listed all the wrongs that were heaped on the head of King George III. I'd ask my students to compare that list of wrongs to the wrong of slavery. And what about women? Were they equal to men in the world of Thomas Jefferson? They could not vote or hold office.

What were the ethical obligations of John Adams and Benjamin Franklin, both of whom were on the committee with Thomas Jefferson to draft that Declaration? They both opposed slavery. Should they have insisted that something be said about slavery or the expectation that it would soon be abolished, or even that slavery was inconsistent with the basic principles of the American Revolution?

Or think about the United States Constitution, which provided for the possibility of a fugitive slave law and counted three-fifths of all "other persons" toward the number of representatives in the House. The Constitution doesn't mention slaves. They are simply "other persons." At least one member of the Constitutional Convention, a Quaker, refused to sign the Constitution because it protected slavery. To create the Union, powerful members of the Convention who opposed slavery—John Adams, Benjamin Franklin, and Alexander Hamilton, among others—held their peace. Should they have? What should they have done? What could they have done and yet forge a Union? Let's get our youngsters thinking in ethical terms. Let them discuss these moral issues. Was the Union worth more than the abolition of slavery?

Turning from history to literature, there are lots of opportunities for a class to discuss ethical issues. One of my favorites is a scene in *Les Misérables*. The heroic Jean Valjean is being hounded by the police officer, Javert, for a minor infraction. Jean Valjean and his little daughter are starving. He enters a church intending to steal two silver candlesticks and sell them to feed his daughter. The priest of the church, watching from behind a curtain, consents silently in his own mind to what Jean Valjean is doing. Is it theft if the priest consents? Does the priest have authority to consent? The candlesticks must have belonged to the church, not the priest. Is unmanifested consent enough to remove the act of Jean Valjean from the felony of theft? Should Javert have hounded Jean Valjean to the point of starving his young daughter? There is a lot for students to talk about in this little scene.

And now to the classics. Iphigenia, the beautiful daughter of Agamemnon, commander of the Greek army, is sacrificed to the goddess Artemis to persuade her to grant the becalmed Greek ships a favorable wind so that they can conquer Troy and bring back Helen—who is living in an adulterous relationship with Paris, son of Priam, King of Troy. Why sacrifice an innocent young woman, Iphigenia, to enable an army to bring back a wayward Helen? Quite apart from the sacrifice of Iphigenia, is a ten-year war justified for the purpose of bringing back Helen of Troy?

In revenge for the killing of their daughter, Agamemnon's wife, Clytemnestra, plots the murder of her husband, and then she in turn is killed by their son, Orestes, to revenge his father's murder. The cycle of revenge is finally ended when Orestes is tried by a jury presided over by the goddess Athena and acquitted because of his repentance. In the end, law prevailed over revenge.

Hamlet is another story about revenge. In seven soliloquies Hamlet himself never once questions whether revenge is the appropriate answer to the murder of his father. And what happens? What fruit does revenge yield? Every major character plus several minor ones are killed violently, including Hamlet himself, the king Claudius, the queen (Hamlet's mother), Laertes, Polonius, Rosencrantz, and Guildenstern. And the crown goes to Fortinbras, King of Norway, Denmark's enemy! What should Hamlet have done once he became satisfied that King Claudius was, in fact, guilty of the murder of his father?

There are also real living situations to which older students can be exposed. They can be taken on a field trip to a court to sit through a criminal trial and then discuss how they would have voted if they had been on the jury. A sentencing hearing is another possibility for testing a person's judgment concerning a crime. Perhaps arrangements could be made with governors' offices to let students sit in on clemency hearings so they could later discuss whether and to what degree they would have granted clemency. Perhaps the officers of some of the community projects designed to help homeless families or persons would agree to talk to ethics classes about their work.

I suggested, therefore, that the local public school authority appoint a committee of school board members to consider whether one class period a week could be devoted to teaching ethics from first through twelfth grades. The committee could hear from teachers and administrators concerning the problems and possibilities of this suggestion. I found from the financial officer of the supervisory union that the cost to the Putney Central School would be about $30,000 a year in a budget of $3.5 million a year.

EPILOGUE

Marion King Schlefer

Epilogue

Marion King Schlefer
1923–2016

Putney, Vermont

THIS OBITUARY APPEARED in the *Brattleboro Reformer* and the *Putney Post*, a magazine published by Marion's alma mater, The Putney School. A shorter version appeared in *The Washington Post*.

Marion King Schlefer, who died on January 17, a month short of her 92nd birthday, was, as her granddaughter Lucy Bicks said, "a woman who taught us to see the beauty in the things humans create"—whether tiles in her bathroom or Antoni Gaudí's Sagrada Família. She conceived all her work, in housing and planning, art and architecture, in Washington, D.C., first of all as good design.

Marion enjoyed Christmas Eve dinner at her house in Putney, Vermont, with her husband of 70 years, Mark P. Schlefer, all of her children, grandchildren, and two sons-in-law. The little Christmas tree was almost smothered in presents. The next day, Christmas morning, her youngest grandchild, Molly Bicks, distributed presents as in past years.

Marion had a pleasant time at Christmas dinner at the nearby house of her daughter and son-in-law, Kate and Charles Dodge. But her strength declined, at first gradually and then sharply, until she died with her entire family around her, except her oldest grandchild, Maggie Dodge, who had to return to her work in Thailand.

Marion was born in Brooklyn Heights, but her family soon moved to Long Island where she grew up, learning to identify birds and flowers. Her father was an engineer on most of the tunnels in and out of Manhattan, and chief engineer of the Lincoln and Brooklyn-Battery tunnels. She graduated from Putney School in 1941, and from Swarthmore College with honors in 1945, and she attended the Harvard Graduate School of Design, and earned a master's degree in art at American University.

Moving to Washington, D.C., Marion was elected to the chair of the Committee of 100 on the Federal City, the oldest planning organization in the city, founded in 1886. She was elected to the board of the Parks and History Association, National Capital Region. She was also a member of the D.C. Board of Commissioners' Planning and Urban Renewal Advisory Council and of the Mayor's Committee on the Downtown, and she received a special tribute at the fiftieth-year celebration of the Metropolitan Washington Planning and Housing Association for distinguished service to the Washington community.

Her major professional work was as an analyst specializing in planning for the Congressional Research Service of the Library of Congress, where she developed ideas, prepared legislation, and wrote background papers on a range of matters, including the New Communities Act [of 1970]. She published studies on industrialized housing, national housing needs, and central-city policies.

During the 1990s, as a member of the board of the Parks and History Association, she was chair of the subcommittee on choosing research projects to be carried out by historians or archeologists within the National Capital Region, for example, concerning various aspects of the operation of the Chesapeake & Ohio Canal, or particular historic buildings or battlefields from the Civil War, or the history of freed slaves during and after the war.

Drawing on her esthetic interests and knowledge, she taught a survey of architecture from Mesopotamia to the Renaissance at Northern Virginia Community College.

She later wrote architectural histories to accompany measured drawings and photographs, which made up the documentation histories of buildings significant for their architecture for the Historic American Buildings Survey for deposit in the Library of Congress. When HABS decided to document parks as well as buildings she was chosen to write the history of two parks: Meridian Hill Park was selected to represent the formal urban park and Dumbarton Oaks to represent the pastoral "naturalistic" park.

Marion had long had close ties to Putney. Her mother bought a farmhouse on the Putney-Dummerston Road in the 1940s. She and her husband, Mark Schlefer, lived in the farmhouse for a year after World War II when he taught American and medieval history at the Putney School and they had a horse, a cow, and 50 chickens. After they retired to Putney in 2005, she was on the boards of Morningside Shelter and Putney Family Services.

She is survived by, in addition to family members mentioned above, a son, Jonathan; a daughter Ellen Schlefer Bicks; and Ellen's husband, Michael Bicks.

Colophon

Incidents in a Life was designed by Denise Arnot of Washington, DC. This text is set in Adobe Caslon, originally designed by William Caslon I (c. 1692–1766) in London. Caslon worked as an engraver of punches, the masters used to stamp the moulds or matrices used to cast metal type. He worked in the tradition of what is now called old-style serif letters, which featured letters with a relatively organic structure resembling handwriting. Caslon established a tradition of engraving type in London. He was influenced by imported Dutch baroque typefaces that were popular in England at the time. His typefaces were admired for their appearance and suitability for extended passages of text.

The sans-serif display type is Nobel, designed by Sjoerd Henrik de Roos (1877–1962) and Dick Dooijes (1909–1998) for the Amsterdam Type foundry. Andrea Fuchs and Fred Smeijers of the Dutch Type Library (DTL) produced a revival in 1993. In the same year, Tobias Frere-Jones, then at Font Bureau, began a revival of the Nobel face in the United States. Cyrus Highsmith and Dyana Weissman later added the light-weight typefaces. Frere-Jones described it as a compromise between the purer geometry of Futura and traditional letters: "Futura cooked in dirty pots and pans."

CPSIA information can be obtained
at www.ICGtesting.com
Printed in the USA
LVHW01s0156020518
575656LV00010B/244/P